# What's for Lunch, Mum?

Gay Firth and Jane Donald were both w
graduating from their respective universi
claimed them.

Gay Firth taught for a time after reading History at Dublin, and has been a part-time feature writer ever since. She has two children, lives in London and commutes constantly to Glasgow.

Jane Donald was a promotion copywriter on *Vogue* magazine and has contributed articles on fashion, travel and mothercraft to various publications. She has four children and lives in Glasgow.

Gay Firth and Jane Donald

# What's for Lunch, Mum?

**Pan Books** in association with
**William Heinemann**

First published 1976 by William Heinemann Ltd
This edition published 1977 by Pan Books Ltd,
Cavaye Place, London SW10 9PG,
in association with William Heinemann Ltd

ISBN 0 330 25031 0
Printed and bound in Great Britain by
Richard Clay (The Chaucer Press) Ltd,
Bungay, Suffolk

# Contents

For our children – and yours

**Note** We assume throughout the basic skills in cookery: sauce-making, seasoning, and keeping children away from the stove. All quantities are for 4 unless otherwise stated. The ingredients are listed in order of use so far as possible; and where flour is mentioned it is Plain unless otherwise stated. Measurements are given in metric and Imperial weights taking 25 grams as the basic unit; and oven temperatures in Fahrenheit, Celsius, and the equivalent in gas markings. Tin sizes vary from product to product; the sizes we indicate have been used by us in cooking the recipes and will, at least, provide guide-lines for readers who can shop for tins that are approximate in size to the ones we recommend.

We give grateful thanks to friends near and far who rallied as one mother to our calls on their experience and expertise; to Julia Nash, our editor; to Rod McLeod, whose cartoons sum up the subject more wittily than words, and to Delia Delderfield for the line drawings in Chapter 6.

# 1 What's for lunch, Mum?

Some women are born cooks, and quite a lot achieve good cookery. All mothers have cooking thrust upon them, and there's no let-up for years and years and years. This is a cookery book for *mothers.* That's all. Anybody else can stop right here, and go off to buy one of those pretty, exciting publications that tell you how to glaze hams so your guests glaze over with admiration; or how to feed fifteen on 50p, or fascinate your husband anew with squid. We're not knocking the nice cookbooks: they are lights to lighten the darkness and we wouldn't be without them. But when we've got kids to feed we don't get round, much, to reading the nice cookbooks much.

For feeding children day after day is a relentless chore. From the day we boast proudly 'he's on Proper Food' we're on a treadmill politely known as Family Meals or Plain Cooking, and it's going to be trouble all the way with psychological warfare thrown in. Mothers learn early that there's more to feeding children than merely keeping them alive.

Cooking for kids isn't difficult; it just gets mothers down. Trotting out wholesome, nutritious, attractive meals to people whose stock response is 'Yuk' is a real strain on our energy and emotions. Children are notoriously conservative about food, too, and so the kind of cooking we get stuck with can be very boring. But most of us feed our children pretty well most of the time. Short of domestic calamity or a mad urge to fly in the face of the law or the social worker, we want to. It's one of those compulsions that go along with motherhood.

Herein is a paradox. Feeding children is the kind of compulsion that can become an obsession, and in our view there is no more dangerous obsession than that which drives a mother to Put Her All into her children's meals. Don't get over-involved. The less soul you put in with the vitamins the less you will mind when the kids don't like it. Or eat it. Or even look at it. Take as little trouble as possible, consistent with your own standards of what is nourishing and tasty, and with the sobering thought that feeding your children well *must* be important to you – or you wouldn't be reading this book. But trying too hard with children's food is the best way we know to ensure that the kids learn to resist both food and Mother. They don't care if you spend five minutes or five hours producing their meals – why should you?

The main meal is the main problem, at least for the first few years. Quiet little suppers are what you have with your husband (yes, a tray in front of the television can be just as civilized as the candle-lit twosome: the acid test is that the children aren't there); preferably cooked from one of those nice cookbooks, not this one. We'll concentrate on children's meals, if you don't mind; and that's what the first four chapters of recipes are all about.

All of us have emergency standbys that ward off starvation when the mind goes blank and little loved ones have to be fed. Packets, tins, mixes, the wide range of frozen foods –

mothers know all about these and it would be cheating to mention them here except as part of a recipe. Our recipes are put together with an eye to the maximum value in taste, time, and cost. If one dish is more expensive or takes a little longer, we say so. So far as cost is concerned, it goes without saying that children are just as likely to smile and eat (or scowl and spit) budget food as they are to drool over expensive stuff like fillet steak, which has no more health advantages than humble stew and is harder to eat.

A monthly rota of recipes for main course, veg, and pudding should satisfy the most capricious child and steady the nerves of the most desperate mother. When you get to the end you can sneak back to the beginning again and hope they won't notice. We're pretty sure they won't, but we can't give any binding guarantees. All the recipes work. That is to say, our kids ate them, which is saying a great deal. One of the many comforts which emerged while putting this book together was the large body of evidence to show that children react with astonishing similarity to similar foods and similar recipes, at least in the English-speaking world. Leaving aside real problems, as distinct from real pigheadedness, most ordinary children start liking stronger tastes some time around the age of four, and ingredients like onion become possible in the cooking. Even garlic need not be regarded as sudden death if you go softly, softly, smiling all the way with garlic salt.

And the left-overs? There are millions of women in the over-nourished western world who are over-weight because they conscientiously eat their children's left-overs. They eat them because they haven't got a dog. Or they eat them because they have a dog, but the dog doesn't like cold macaroni. We eat them, and we bet you do too. We try not to, and so, hopefully, do you.

We're not going to add yet another to the huge catalogue of cookbook chapters on left-overs, which are the most depressing kind of reading anyway. Rather we have trickled suggestions through the pages as left-overs happened to come up. There are as many philosophies about them as there are mothers, but the following notion is too good to leave out. The most waste-conscious mother we know invented, tested and sent us a recipe for what she bravely calls 'a fine rough jam'. You collect all apple cores and/or half-eaten apples, half-sucked oranges and/or orange peel and a handful of any soft fruit in season: she prefers not-very-nice blackberries. Then you put it all in a saucepan (don't overdo the orange, she says), cover with water and simmer till mushy. Strain or liquidize, then add a pound of sugar for every pint and go ahead as usual.

If dealing with left-overs takes imagination, feeding children successfully and happily takes a combination of confidence and confidence trickery known only to mothers, and then known only to some. There are – there must be – golden mothers who lavish time and intelligence on their children's meals with unshakeable pleasure and never a passing sigh for the lack of appreciation. All honour and glory to them. The rest of us have days when we think we shall run amok in the instant mixes if we have to think up, cook, and live through one more meal. This book is for those days.

# 2 Main course

Mince moves in mysterious ways – or if kids will eat meat at all, they'll eat mince. We defy a mother to do without it, and mums are welcome to defy us to mince the meat ourselves. We don't. (Cooked meats are something else again and here a mincer comes in very handy.) It's usually cheaper and probably more reliable to mince raw meat at home, but the time and mess come too high for an ingredient as staple as this one. Butchers do a perfectly adequate beef mince at a fair price and a rather better, more expensive one which is nice for hamburgers and meat-balls that need quick cooking to be really good and juicy. The adequate kind is the one we're using here, in a selection of recipes to add to everybody's well-worn repertoire.

### Munchy mince

500 g (1 lb) mince
2 large onions, chopped
1 medium tin (298 g or 10½ oz) condensed oxtail soup
100 g (4 oz) grated cheese
salt and pepper, if necessary

From the beginning, now, and for ever more, dried onion flakes or pieces should be taken as read as an honourable substitute for the real thing. They save a lot of tears, both from you and the children. Use according to the directions on the packet.

Brown the mince and onion in a casserole in a little fat, then remove from the heat and stir in the undiluted soup and the grated cheese. Season, cover, and bake at 275°F (140°C or gas 1) for about an hour.

### Crunchy mince

This one has mushrooms in it, and some kids don't like mushrooms. If yours don't, just keep quiet and they won't even notice. It's that kind of recipe, unless your kids are the kind who can pick out a mushroom in the middle of an eclipse.

1 chopped onion
100 g (4 oz) chopped mushrooms
500 g (1 lb) mince
4 small packets of crisps, crushed
salt and pepper
175 ml (7 fl oz) milk (approx) with 1 egg beaten into it
50 g (2 oz) grated cheese

Chop the onion and mushrooms and fry gently together with the mince. Add three-quarters of the crushed crisps. Season, then press the mixture into a greased pie dish or loaf tin and pour the egg-and-milk over the top. Bake uncovered for 45 minutes at 375°F (190°C or gas 5). Then sprinkle with the grated cheese and remaining crisps and bake for another 10 minutes while you wash everybody's hands.

### Dutch roast

1 thick slice of bread
125 ml (5 fl oz or ¼ pint) milk
500 g (1 lb) mince
1 finely chopped onion
salt and pepper
1 egg
a few knobs of butter or marge

Cut off the crusts and soak the bread in the milk for 10 minutes (or more, or less: it just has to be soggy). Mash it well with a fork or potato masher, mix in the mince and onion and season well. (Note here that only you know how much salt and pepper your children will take without moaning, so taste and season accordingly.) Beat the egg and stir into the mixture, then turn into a greased fireproof dish or casserole, level off the top and dab on the bits of butter. Cover and bake in a moderate oven, 325°F (170°C or gas 3) for about an hour. Scots mums with Mac or Mc in their name serve this hot with turnips; and so can you, so there.

**Meter mince**

Every mother needs a good reliable mince recipe that she can hurl into the oven and leave without a backward glance. This one will stand a half-hour delay better than a parking meter, and it's cheaper than the fine you mustn't get.

500 g (1 lb) thinly sliced potatoes
1 chopped onion
500 g (1 lb) mince
a pinch of dried herbs (optional)
1 medium tin (283 g or 10 oz) peas or green beans, or left-over green veg
1 medium tin (298 g or 10½ oz) condensed mushroom soup
salt and pepper
a few dabs of butter or margarine

Boil the sliced potatoes for 5 minutes and drain well. Fry the onion for 5 minutes, add the mince and herbs, then fry all together for 10 minutes. Now drain off the fat and add the drained green vegetables and the undiluted soup. Season and put it all into a casserole, arrange the potato slices over the top and scatter on the butter or marge. Meanwhile you have heated the oven to 275°F (140°C or gas 1). Put your coat on, put the uncovered casserole in the oven, and you're clear for an hour and perhaps a little longer if you simply must try on that dress.

**Chilly child chili**

Children are suspicious of anything you cook for them that is not instantly recognizable as a trusty friend. Fancy names put them off like nobody's business, too: they say 'What's this?' and if you say brightly 'Lovely chili!' there is a chorus of banshee wails and they won't even look at it. A safe rule of thumb is never to answer the question in the first place. As you put the dish on the table you can cut off the What's This at the draw if you start talking about anything other than food and go on talking right through lunch. It's a big strain, but the second time around the kids will probably swallow this good recipe without the monologue.

500 g (1 lb) mince
1 large chopped onion
1 medium tin (283 g or 10 oz) broad beans or 1 large packet frozen or 250 g (½ lb) fresh
1 medium tin (298 g or 10½ oz) condensed tomato soup
1 teaspoon (a little more than level) chili powder
a little salt and pepper

Fry the mince and onion for 10 minutes and then add all the other ingredients (make sure you drain the beans). Season and let the whole thing simmer for three-quarters of an hour. Or transfer the mixture to a casserole, cover it, and bake it in the oven for an hour at 275°F (140°C or gas 1). Dish up and make with the chat.

### Mock moussaka

375 g (¾ lb) mince
2 chopped onions
250 g (½ lb) tomatoes or 1 small tin (226 g or 8 oz)
500 g (1 lb) peeled and sliced potatoes, parboiled for 10 minutes

*Sauce*

10-15 g (½ oz) margarine
10-15 g (½ oz) flour
250 ml (½ pint) milk
1 egg
25 g (1 oz) grated cheese
salt and pepper

Fry the mince and onion lightly brown, then add the tomatoes (if fresh, peel, see page 42, and chop). Now season. Put a layer of sliced partly-cooked potatoes in a casserole, then a layer of mince mixture, and repeat as many times as the stuff will hold out, finishing with a layer of potatoes. Make the sauce with the marge, flour, and milk, remove from heat and stir in the lightly beaten egg and the cheese. Mix well and pour over the casserole. Bake uncovered at 375°F (190°C or gas 5) for an hour. The top should be nicely browned, and you can have a nice stimulating conversation at lunch about Greece and the Greeks, who eat real moussaka and love it.

**Hamburg heaven**

One of the reasons why our hamburgers tend to fall apart in the cooking is that we're mean and won't use Best Mince. It helps if you do, but any hamburger any time is usually popular, especially if you pull out all the stops and serve them in hot baps or buns. And ketchup – some kids will eat anything if it comes with ketchup. One efficient mum rolls out a double quantity of this hamburger recipe into a large sausage shape, chills it, slices it, and stores the surplus in the freezer. It's nice if you have a deep freeze, but if you don't it is very far from being the end of your world.

375 g (¾ lb) mince
1 finely chopped onion
1 egg
salt and pepper
seasoned flour

Mix the mince and onion together and season well. Break in the egg and mix like mad to bind everything together – mixing with the hand is more effective than with a spoon and you're going to get messy anyway because you now have to form the mixture into flattened rounds. Roll these in the seasoned flour and fry fast till brown on both sides. They should be pink and juicy in the middle and will keep hot in a covered dish in a slow oven if you're making a big batch. Heat the buns through in the oven while you're cooking.

**Battered mince**

You can use mince left-overs here, and if you're using fresh mince a little will go a long way.

250 g (½ lb) mince
1 small chopped onion
125 ml (5 fl oz or ¼ pint) water or stock
salt and pepper

*Batter*

50 g (2 oz) margarine
100 g (4 oz) self-raising flour
1 egg
125 ml (5 fl oz or ¼ pint) milk

Season the mince and onion and fry together for 10 minutes, then stir in the water or stock and transfer to a greased casserole. (It will not have escaped you that you can often do all meat cooking for children in one casserole – mixing, frying, baking – and it saves a lot of wear and tear and washing up.)

Make the batter by rubbing the marge into the flour until it looks like breadcrumbs, then add the egg and beat well, putting in the milk a little at a time as you go along. Pour the batter over the mince mixture and bake uncovered at 375°F (190°C or gas 5) for just under an hour. The batter puffs up like Yorkshire pudding and makes the dish look more impressive than it really is.

### Meat loaf mother-in-law

The great thing about meat loaf is that you can double or treble it, eat it hot or eat it cold, dress it up or dress it down. Children usually like it as much as adults and there's no better way of demonstrating to your mother-in-law that her grandchildren are receiving the utmost in love, care, and good food. If she comes on a Tuesday and you have roast lamb with all the trimmings she won't be fooled for a moment – she'll know you're doing it for effect and will suspect habitual neglect. Give her a good meat loaf and she'll feel bad about all the nasty thoughts she's had about you all these years, even to the point of telling her friends what a Good Little Mother you are. This is a good loaf. The breadcrumbs are a nuisance, but worth it.

375 g ($\frac{3}{4}$ lb) mince
250 g ($\frac{1}{2}$ lb) bacon (any cut) minced or cut fine with kitchen scissors
250 g ($\frac{1}{2}$ lb) fresh white breadcrumbs
125 ml (5 fl oz or $\frac{1}{4}$ pint) milk
2 eggs
1 tablespoon (25 g or 1 oz) brown sugar
1 teaspoon dry mustard
salt and pepper

Mix the mince and bacon together while you soak the breadcrumbs in the milk. Now beat the eggs with the mustard, stir into the milk-and-crumb mixture and tip it all into the meats. Mix all together and season well. Grease a loaf tin (don't miss out the corners or the finished article will come out like the dog's dinner, all jagged edges). Sprinkle the base with brown sugar, then press in the loaf mixture. Cover with a loose wrapping of baking foil and bake for 1½ hours at 300°F (150°C or gas 2), while you frantically clear up the house and locate the presents she gave the kids last Christmas. (Remember to brush your hair before she arrives.) When the loaf is cooked, ease a knife slowly and thoroughly round the tin to loosen it and turn out on to a hot meat dish. Serve surrounded by a purée of peas (see Vegetables page 36) or grilled tomatoes, or any ostentatiously vitamin-packed vegetable you can rely on your children to eat.

You'll notice that we haven't said a word about Shepherd's Pie, Cottage Pie, or even plain Boiled Mince. We're not going to, either. Those are for the really bad days when you can't even think straight, let alone open a cookery book.

So much for mince. Let us move on to the Stews, and as a stepping stone here is a useful recipe for dumplings, which a lot of kids like and which make stews go further.

### Dad's dumplings

- 150 g (6 oz) flour
- 1½ level teaspoons baking powder
- 35 g (1½ oz) suet or margarine
- ½ teaspoon salt
- pinch of dried herbs (optional, but nice)
- cold water

Mix the dry ingredients together including the suet. (Margarine should be rubbed in.) Now dribble in the cold water and mix to a firm light dough. Divide into small, equal-sized balls and add to any stew 25 minutes before the end of the total cooking time.

It is widely believed that you can put a stew into a slow oven and forget about it. So you can, but over-cooked stews are slimy and can put children off.

The cheaper the meat the longer the cooking time, and the amount saved on the meat allegedly outweighs the increases in your fuel bill. Butchers usually have two or three cuts of stewing steak at different prices, and the cheapest can be very tough indeed, besides being criss-crossed with sinews. This takes longer preparation and longer, careful cooking if children's plates are not to be decorated with unattractive hunks of semi-chewed gristle at the end of a meal. The kind of stewing meat you buy depends on your personal budget, but in any case we should point out that a good pair of kitchen scissors is better and quicker for cutting meat than the so-called sharp knife. Cut meat *small* for children. Oversized bites depress them, and since many are too lazy to chew at all you want at least to ensure that the meat goes down in small bits rather than choky lumps that play havoc with their digestion.

Stewing beef, lamb or mutton, and the cheaper cuts of pork and veal all make good economical stews. The basic method is the time-honoured routine of tossing chopped meat in seasoned flour, frying it brown in dripping or any fat and putting it in a casserole with onion and any root vegetable, then pouring in water-and-beef-extract or stock. Cooking time runs between 2 and 4 hours at 275°F (140°C or gas 1), depending on the quality of the meat. Since there are as many ways of making stews as there are of playing roulette, try this one.

**Russian roulette**

500 g (1 lb) stewing beef or mutton
1 large tin (425 g or 15 oz) baked beans
1 medium tin (298 g or 10½ oz) condensed tomato soup
a pinch of dried herbs
garlic salt if you can get away with it
salt and pepper

Cut up the meat and fry lightly brown in a casserole. Stir in the tin of beans and the undiluted soup. Throw in the herbs and garlic salt and go easy on any other seasoning, because this stew doesn't need much. Cover and cook in a slow oven, 275°F (140°C or gas 1), for 2-4 hours. This is a good recipe to double up for a big Saturday midday meal.

**Speedy stew**

This takes no fewer than 5 tins, but before the cash register starts ringing remember your left-overs. Left-over stew with tins of veg and vice versa; and of course you can use fresh vegetables if you time them to fit in with the total cooking time. Carrots and potatoes take an hour to stew, celery a little less than an hour, most green vegetables 20 minutes or so. But if you're really in a hurry this is a quick hot-pot that works.

1 tin (425 g or 15 oz) stewing steak
1 tin (298 g or 10½ oz) sliced carrots
1 tin (298 g or 10½ oz) sliced green beans
1 tin (298 g or 10½ oz) green peas
1 tin (538 g or 1 lb 3 oz) new potatoes
salt and pepper
knobs of butter or marge

Mix everything except the potatoes in a casserole and season. Drain the potatoes and arrange them on top. Scatter over the knobs of butter and bake uncovered for about half an hour at 375°F (190°C or gas 5), by which time the potatoes should be lightly browned.

It's terrible to tell lies, but when you're a mother cooking for children you have to face the fact that the only useful thing about a principle is that it can be sacrificed to expediency. (That's what mothers and politicians have in common.) A lady we know chalked up a resounding success with curry by telling her children that the funny taste was nuts. The kids liked nuts. She liked curry, and she wanted them to like it too. She started with a cautious teaspoonful of curry powder, increasing gradually to a bold tablespoonful until the entire family was eating curries that would blister a Bengali. She calls it curry now, and can't or won't remember how she eased into the truth. Here it is, and you can make it either with mince or with stewing beef or lamb.

**Caroline's nutty curry**

500 g (1 lb) stewing beef (or mince or stewing lamb)
1 large onion
a small packet dried vegetables (packet vegetable soup will do)
a handful of sultanas
1 dessertspoon cornflour
1 level dessertspoon mild curry powder (up to 3 if you dare)
500 ml (1 pint) stock made with water and a beef stock cube
salt and pepper

Chop the meat and onion and put them in a casserole with the veg and sultanas. Now mix the cornflour and curry powder together, stir in the pint of stock and pour this sauce into the dish. Season, cover, and cook in a slow oven, 275°F (140°C, gas 1) for 2-4 hours, depending on the kind of meat you're using. Serve with rice and stick to your principles until (as with many a politician) they look like spelling your ruin. Then be ready with the well-rehearsed lie.

**Very easy veal**

Stewing veal comes in pallid lumps which look as if they could come from anywhere. Not all butchers have it, but if you can locate the stuff it makes a good stew, enormously improved in flavour by the addition of bacon.

500 g (1 lb) stewing veal
250 g (½ lb) bacon (any cut)
250 g (½ lb) sliced carrots
50 g (2 oz) seasoned flour
500 ml (1 pint) chicken stock (or a stock cube with water)
salt and pepper

Cut up the veal and bacon, toss the pieces in seasoned flour and fry together in a casserole till lightly brown. Mix in the sliced carrots and stir in the stock. The bacon in this dish makes it salty, so taste before adding any other seasoning. Cover and bake in a slow oven, 275°F (140°C or gas 1) for 2½ hours. (If you have time and strength you can make a proper sauce for stew: rub 50 g (2 oz) marge into 50 g (2 oz) flour, mix in the stock and pour over the fried meats and veg. Double this and save the surplus for handy gravy next day.)

**Pig-in-a-poke** (for 6)

Pork isn't the easiest meat to give children and the sight of a pork chop sitting large and solid on a plate can be daunting. It sounds extravagant to use pork fillet, but there's no waste, it's tender, it tastes good, and we think it's fair value. It makes the kind of casserole you can cheerfully serve up to discerning adults as well, so save it for weekends.

1 whole pork fillet
2 chopped onions
50 g (2 oz) seasoned flour
375 ml (¾ pint) milk-and-stock mixture

1 tub (125 ml or 5 fl oz) plain yoghurt or sour cream
3 apples, peeled and diced
a little black pepper

Cut the pork fillet into pieces and toss these in seasoned flour, then fry in dripping with the chopped onion and put in a casserole. Stir in the milk-and-stock and check the seasoning – this dish can be too bland and a little black pepper is good if you can risk it. Cook covered in a moderate oven, 350°F (180°C or gas 4) for an hour, then mix in the yoghurt and diced apple and bake again for 15-20 minutes.

### Cheeky cheese chops

There is a time in a child's life when one lamb chop is not enough and two are too many; like daytime naps for toddlers. One answer to the problem is to hide the exact number of chops with a good filling sauce, so that second helpings can be a tablespoon of cheesy stuff, even though the chops are finished.

4 lamb chops or cutlets
1 medium tin (298 g or 10½ oz) condensed celery soup
salt and pepper
100 g (4 oz) grated cheese
2 level tablespoons fine breadcrumbs (use packet ones)

Grill the chops for 5-6 minutes on either side, then put them in a shallow ovenproof dish and spoon the undiluted soup over them. Sprinkle on a little salt and pepper, then pile the grated cheese and crumbs on top and put back under the grill. In 4 or 5 minutes the cheese will have melted and the top will be brown and crisp.

If you're cooking this for under-fives, bake the uncooked chops with the soup and cheese in a covered casserole at 300°F (150°C or gas 2) for about an hour. This way the meat will be more tender and easier to chew.

### **Paddy's pot** (for 8)

It is almost unknown for children, or anyone else, to do a thumbs down on Irish stew. The bigger the pot the better it tastes and, like the Troubles in Ireland, there's always a bit left over to boil up again later. Ideally you need a huge cast-iron casserole or cauldron, but the biggest saucepan in the house will do fine. The ingredients are infinitely variable but it's nice if there is as much meat as veg. Parsnips and/or turnips could be sliced in with the carrots, and if the kids like a thicker gravy you can juggle in some flour or cornflour, but pearl barley will do the thickening trick if you put in a lot.

1-1½ kg (2-3 lb) stewing lamb or mutton, bones and all
1 kg (2 lb) peeled whole potatoes
500 g (1 lb) thickly sliced carrots
2 or 3 large sliced onions
150 g (6 oz) pearl barley, or more for a thicker stew
salt and pepper
water

Wipe over the meat, prepare the vegetables and dump the whole lot into your largest saucepan with the pearl barley and seasoning. Pour in cold water to cover. Bring to the boil, and skim the top when it gets scummy-looking. Now taste – it might need more salt. Cover and simmer for at least 2 hours until the meat is tender and starts to fall off the bones. Serve in bowls, with a spare plate on the table for discarded bones, and give everybody spoons as well as forks.

**Lovely liver loaf**

Offal is nutritious and most kids hate it and that's life. Here's a recipe for liver which is messy to make but which often succeeds where all others have failed.

250 g (½ lb) liver (any kind: ox is cheapest and lamb nicest)
100 g (4 oz) pork sausage meat
50 g (2 oz) rindless bacon
1 onion
2 slices of white bread
1 egg
125 ml (5 fl oz or ¼ pint) water
a little salt and pepper

Put the liver, sausage meat, bacon, peeled onion, and bread through the mincer. Now beat the egg with the water and stir well into the mixture (it needs very little seasoning). Press into a greased loaf tin and bake uncovered for about 50 minutes at 375°F (190°C or gas 5). If the kids still kick and scream try it cold, spread on crackers.

**Corny hash** (for 4-6)

A tin or two of corned beef is an essential standby. When the rain pours down and you'd rather die than set foot out of the house this hash will make you feel you've done your duty by the kids and they'd better play quietly all afternoon Or Else.

2 chopped onions
1 340 g (12 oz) tin corned beef
4 tomatoes, peeled and chopped (or a small tin)
3 meat cubes
500 g (1 lb) potatoes, cooked and mashed
a few knobs of butter or marge
salt and pepper

Fry up the onions and add the chopped corned beef, tomatoes and crumbled meat cubes. Season, then fry all together for a few minutes. Put a layer of mashed potato in a casserole, a layer of hash on top, and so on until you run out, finishing with a layer of potato. Dot the butter over the top and cook uncovered in a hot oven, 400°F (200°C or gas 6) for 20-30 minutes.

Taking stock for a moment, that's more than two weeks' worth of main courses for midday meals and they all use *meat*. Only a few require anything but the minimum in time and brainpower. None of them need the kind of expensive ingredients that lead a mother to put most of her heart into cooking and then break what remains of it when faced with the left-overs. Most important, while you wouldn't exactly fall over with joy if you met them at an adult dinner party, we'd like to think you might actually fancy them yourself. Mothers who sit down for a sociable meal with children deserve nice food. When you're jumping up and down like a yo-yo to retrieve forks from under the table and grab a spilling jug you're entitled to some consideration. Whether you eat lunch or not is beside the point, but we hope you do. Too many mothers don't have proper meals and get fat anyway on the left-overs. That's a recurring hazard; and so is *Fish*, which comes up now.

The discovery that nine children out of ten won't come to grips with fish is like the discovery that you can't come to grips with the New Maths – you keep going back to the beginning in the hope that you'll get there in the end. (Fish holds out more hope than New Maths in that most people do seem to come round to it eventually.) The mother whose child actually likes fish should spend time in silent, grateful prayer. The rest of us just suffer, but there are a few life-saving exceptions to the general rule.

The first is fish-and-chips. Chips are the big attraction here, of course, but we find that almost anything deep-fried in batter and cooking oil is pretty popular. (See Puddings, page 60, for a good batter, and remember to leave out the sugar.) If you can establish the idea that fish means chips too, and your kids never get chips *except* with fish (like love and marriage . . .) you may do well for a while. Eventually the children will catch on that this is no magic formula and bang goes your credibility and, probably, the fish.

The second exception is that any child who catches a fish all by himself will eat it and love it. Since this is likely to mean a lot of expensive equipment, to say nothing of falling into rivers, lochs, and seas while you stand in terror and a freezing wind on the shore, forget it.

And on the third day somebody said 'Let there be Tuna', and there was tuna. And the kids ate it and wanted more. Tuna is to fish as mince is to meat – a theme upon which you can play variations and now and again a whole symphony. It is fairly cheap, it comes in tins and it has no bones. We find it hard to do without.

Some time ago there was a Great Tinned Tuna Scare during which many mothers were scared off tuna. A few still believe that merely to have a tin in the house is enough to bring the whole family down with mercury poisoning. We've had the Great Corned Beef Scare too, and the Cyclamates-in-Fruit-Juice Scare, and one way and another it's a wonder we're all alive. The point about exposing any hazard which might be present in processed food of any kind is that from that moment on, manufacturers and distributors fall over backwards to avoid getting caught out again. On the whole our chances of living to a ripe old age get better and better and so do our children's. The way to avoid further scandals, which may or may not be lurking under the surface of tranquil eating, is to join a consumer group and go right on buying tuna on the principle that the safest time to fly is after a crash. Justified concern is one thing, but alarm and despondency over all things tinned is as much a hazard to health as the occasional scientific slip-up.

### Kids' kedgeree

125 g (5 oz) rice (the long-grain kind)
1 tin (184 g or 6½ oz) tuna fish
1 medium tin (298 g or 10½ oz) condensed mushroom soup
50 g (2 oz) grated cheese
a squeeze of lemon juice
salt and pepper

Boil the rice in plenty of salted water for about 15 minutes while you're opening tins and flaking the tuna. Drain the rice well, mix in the undiluted soup and then the tuna, with the dash of lemon juice and seasoning. Scatter the grated cheese over the top and bake uncovered for 20 minutes or so in a medium oven, 300°F (150°C or gas 2) to heat the dish through and melt the cheese.

Watch now. If your children eat this a few times you can try some cooked fresh haddock or cod mixed in with less tuna and see what happens. You could also use tomato soup instead of mushroom – it tastes stronger and more effectively disguises the fish. And here's what to do with left-over tuna.

### Tuneful tuna

1 tin (184 g or 6½ oz) tuna, or a smaller tin, or left-overs
100 g (4 oz) cooked macaroni or spaghetti (or more, to spin out the dish)
1 medium tin (298 g or 10½ oz) condensed chicken soup
4 tablespoons fresh white breadcrumbs
a few dabs of butter or marge
salt and pepper

Mix together the tuna, pasta, soup, and seasoning in a greased casserole. Top with the crumbs, dot with the butter or marge and bake uncovered for 30 minutes at 375°F (190°C or gas 5).

The next three look pretty and offer wide scope for using

honest-to-God fish as well as or instead of tuna. A mixture of tuna and cooked fresh haddock (cod, kipper, mackerel, and more expensive fish like plaice will all do) is fair to the child who thinks of 'fish' as that alarmingly real creature with a tail and googly eyes in his nature book. (If the beef we buy were habitually called 'cow' a lot of us would cringe as we ate it; and 'pig' instead of pork or bacon doesn't bear thinking about.) Getting all the bones out of fish is like getting needles out of haystacks, and there's always that one needle left to spite you; but it's a worthy cause.

**Tuna-in-a-blanket** (for 4-6)

226 g (8 oz) frozen puff pastry
1 tin (184 g or 6½ oz) tuna (or equivalent in cooked fresh fish)
3 peeled and chopped tomatoes (or a small tin)
3 chopped hard-boiled eggs
salt and pepper

Roll the pastry into a large rectangle. Flake the tuna or whatever fish mixture you're using and mix it up with the tomatoes and eggs and some seasoning. Brush the pastry with water, spread the mixture over the lower half, fold over the top flap and seal down the edges. Bake in a hot oven, 400°F (200°C or gas 6) for 20 minutes. This amount will make up to six individual pasties, but who wants to do that when one is quicker?

**Tuna soufflé**

1 small tin tuna (if you're using real fish add a little more than the equivalent weight – tuna is filling and a little goes a long way)
25 g (1 oz) margarine
25 g (1 oz) flour
125 ml (5 fl oz or ¼ pint) milk
3 separated eggs
salt and pepper

Mash the fish. Now make a thick sauce with the marge, flour, and milk. Stir in the egg yolks one at a time, then stir in the fish and season well. Beat the egg whites stiff, then fold into the mixture and pour into a small greased soufflé dish or a casserole. Bake for 30 minutes at 400°F (200°C or gas 6). There's no magic about making soufflés, but the rosy glow of actually creating one for your children will stay with you for hours.

### Tuna mousse

2 tins (184 g or 6½ oz) tuna fish or 500 g (1 lb) cooked fresh fish
150 g (6 oz) chopped celery or lettuce
1 teaspoon vinegar
125 ml (5 fl oz or ¼ pint) salad cream
1 packet gelatine (10 g or ½ oz)
3 tablespoons water
salt and pepper

Mix the fish, celery, vinegar, and salad cream together, and season lightly. Now warm 3 tablespoons of water in a small thick pan and add the gelatine powder. Stir until the gelatine dissolves and the mixture is clear. Mix this into the fish mixture. Rinse a mould, a casserole or a dainty glass dish with cold water, pour in the mixture and leave to set. This will keep in the refrigerator for a day or so, and you can always share it with another mother when she drops in to bore you to death about her family's food fads.

### Poor mum's salmon

When the housekeeping is running low and there's no left-over in sight you can put a good face on things with the cheapest tin of salmon.

1 tin (184 g or 6½ oz) salmon
2 sticks celery, finely chopped
2 tablespoons lemon juice
75 g (3 oz) white breadcrumbs
a few knobs of butter or marge
salt and pepper

*Sauce*

25 g (1 oz) marge
25 g (1 oz) flour
1 large tin (425 g or 15 oz) evaporated milk
2 level teaspoons dry mustard

Flake the salmon and chop the celery pretty fine. Make a rich white sauce with the marge, flour, and undiluted evaporated milk. Boil up the sauce, stirring well, and season before mixing in the salmon, celery, and lemon juice. Turn into a greased casserole, top with breadcrumbs and put on the dabs of butter or marge. Bake uncovered at 375°F (190°C or gas 5) for about half-an-hour.

But it is carrying tins too far to abandon fish without so much as a stab at the real McCoy. These individual fish parcels have been known to appeal to children on presentation alone.

### Foiled again fish

4 fillets of any white fish (plaice, whiting, haddock, cod)
100 g (4 oz) mushrooms
4 tomatoes, skinned and chopped (or a small tin)
50 g (2 oz) shrimps (optional)
4 knobs butter
lemon juice
salt and pepper

Cut four generous squares of baking foil and grease each one. Roll up each fillet and lay on a square, then add some tomato, mushroom, and shrimp to each one. Season well and moisten with a drip of lemon juice. Dot with butter, then make a parcel of each square and bake for 25 minutes at 350°F (180°C or gas 4). Serve the parcels unopened, and if a howl of disappointment goes up try not to think too badly of us. We're all in the same boat with fish.

### Prawn perhaps

The minor mention of shrimps in the previous recipe is a major matter. Some kids like shellfish in small quantities, some find them rubbery and won't eat them; a few react violently and get upset, sometimes actually ill. Only trial and error can establish who those few are going to be. It's better to find out early and at home, before a friend makes the mistake on your behalf and you cherish the grudge to your grave. This recipe makes the best of a few prawns and is a good try-out.

1 medium tin (298 g or 10½ oz) condensed tomato soup
125 ml (5 fl oz or ¼ pint) milk
10 g (½ oz) butter
100 g (4 oz) prawns (fresh, frozen, or tinned)
50 g (2 oz) grated cheese
100 g (4 oz) cooked and drained macaroni
salt and pepper

Heat the soup in a saucepan and stir in the milk, butter, prawns, and cheese. Now mix in the macaroni and seasoning. When the whole mixture is hot, dish it on to warm plates. (If you want to make this in advance and reheat it, use a little more milk, then put the mixture in a greased casserole topped with brown breadcrumbs and extra cheese. Bake uncovered for 20 minutes in a moderate oven, 300°F (150°C or gas 2).

**Fish finger final**

Frozen fish fingers grilled or fried straight out of their packet are the quickest and surest way to get kids to eat fish. They are also about the most expensive way – why give packers all the pennies? If the idea of making your own hasn't occurred to you (or if it has occurred to you and you had a fit of the vapours at the very idea) then proceed as follows and get ready for a surprise.

500 g (1 lb) any white fish (cod and haddock are good) bought in a slab or thick fillet
150 g (6 oz) seasoned flour
1 egg beaten into 125 ml (5 fl oz or ¼ pint) of milk

Cut the fish into finger-shaped wedges and take out any bones you see. Dip each finger in the seasoned flour, then in the egg-and-milk, then in the seasoned flour *again*. Now deep-fry them (see page 45) in cooking oil for 10-15 minutes. Drain them on paper and locate the ketchup. The surprise is that it's that simple; and you will be even more surprised when you find out how good they are – and as good cold.

As a last gasp, though, instant fish fingers cannot be sneered at by any mother in a hurry. You can fancy them up this way if it makes you feel better.

**Handy fingers**

10 fish fingers
1 medium tin (298 g or 10½ oz) condensed celery or mushroom soup
125 ml (5 fl oz or ¼ pint) milk
1 tablespoon lemon juice
75 g (3 oz) grated cheese
chopped chives or parsley (optional)
salt and pepper

Lay the fingers in a shallow greased casserole. Thin the soup with the milk, add the cheese and lemon juice; check the seasoning, and pour over the fish. Sprinkle on the chives or parsley, cover, and bake for 20 minutes at 425°F (220°C or gas 7) or 30 minutes at 350°F (180°C or gas 4) if the fingers are still completely frozen. If there is a whine for fish fingers 'the old way, mum', count to ten and remember Van Gogh wasn't appreciated either.

But there is not, repeat not, anything fishy about *Chicken*.

Chicken has become one of the great moral issues of our time. For years every food connoisseur has hammered out the message that today's chicken (the battery chicken, the frozen chicken) is as far removed from the cosy clucking lady of the good old days as kids' left-overs are from lunch at the Savoy Grill. Chicken isn't bred the same, it isn't fed the same, it doesn't taste the same. It's a plastic-wrapped phoney and we all ought to be ashamed of ourselves.

All perfectly reasonable and probably true, but before anyone bursts into tears there are one or two points worth remembering. Chicken nowadays is a great deal cheaper than the old-fashioned farm-bred bird. By the time the old-fashioned chicken farmer had chased his flock of squawking hysterics round the yard, caught them, killed them, plucked them, and marketed them in the good old-fashioned way, they came pretty expensive even for the old-fashioned budget, and if you insist on this kind of pedigree they still are.

Just as important from our point of view is the fact that squawk though the purists may, the taste of modern chicken might have been invented by a mother for her children. It is bland. It is inoffensive. It doesn't taste much of anything, and that's what children like. To make chicken taste of anything you have to put other things with it, and lo, you can. By all means take an outraged tone when discussing the chicken issue with adult gourmets, but don't duck the main chance when it comes to feeding the kids.

Of course you can roast it. It's not marvellous, but it's pretty nice just the same. If you remember to spread some dripping or marge over the breast and legs and then sprinkle on some dry mustard and salt, it will taste even nicer and you'll get the basis of a good gravy. You can skip the regular stuffing and roast it with an onion inside. You can boil it with vegetables and bake it in more ways than there are arguments about it, and still the children will put up no more serious protest than 'Chicken *again*?'. Here are five ideas about what to do with it.

### Broiler bravura

4 chopped rashers streaky bacon
2 chopped onions (optional but preferable)
1 small tin (226 g or 8 oz) tomatoes
1 bayleaf or a few dried herbs (optional)
1 small chicken or 4 chicken joints
salt and pepper

Lightly fry the bacon and onion together, then add the tomatoes and herbs, and season. Fry the chicken on all sides if you feel you must, but it can go into a casserole without the tan. Pour over the sauce, then cover and bake for 1½ hours in a moderate oven, 350°F (180°C or gas 4). Tomatoes are excellent with chicken, but you can ring all kinds of other changes with sweetcorn, diced vegetables, more or less anything that comes to hand.

### Fowl flan

This means baking a pastry case (or not – see page 87 for Cracker flan). What you lose on the swings you gain on the roundabouts, because you can use left-over chicken for this and no-one will know.

1 20 cm (8 in.) flan case
100 g (4 oz) chopped fried bacon
50 g (2 oz) mushrooms
150 g (6 oz) chopped cooked chicken

*Sauce*
25 g (1 oz) margarine
25 g (1 oz) flour
250 ml (10 fl oz or ½ pint) milk or a mixture of milk and chicken stock
1 separated egg
salt and pepper

Fry up the bacon bits with the mushrooms. Now make a thick white sauce with the marge, flour, and liquid and stir in the egg yolk. Season the sauce, then mix in the chicken, bacon, and mushroom. Beat the egg white stiffly and fold it into the mixture, then pour it all into the flan case and bake for 30 minutes at 400°F (200°C or gas 6).

**Dolly-bird bake**

1 tin (280 g or 10 oz) drained asparagus (or peas, or beans, or corn)
250 g (8 oz) chopped cooked chicken
1 medium tin (298 g or 10½ oz) condensed mushroom soup
2 tablespoons milk
salt and pepper
50 g (2 oz) grated cheese
50 g (2 oz) fresh white breadcrumbs

Grease a casserole and arrange the drained vegetables over the base. Scatter the chopped chicken on top, then pour over the soup mixed with the milk and seasoning. Mix the grated cheese with the breadcrumbs and sprinkle them over the top of the dish, then bake uncovered for 30 minutes at 400°F (200°C or gas 6).

**Swell joints**

4 chicken joints
1 medium tin (298 g or 10½ oz) condensed mushroom or celery soup
salt and pepper

This is about as exciting as a swollen knee but the kids won't care, and you can sit down very soon. Brown the joints all over and put them in a casserole with any diced left-over vegetables around. Pour over the soup, season, cover and bake at 350°F (180°C or gas 4) while you put your feet up for 45 minutes.

**Chicken licken** (for 6)

If you put this together on Saturday you can enjoy Sunday morning with the papers and have a good meal with no effort.

2 large tins (482 g or 1 lb) drained leaf spinach (or equivalent fresh or frozen)
150 g (6 oz) grated cheese
150 g (6 oz) cooked long-grain rice
375 g (12 oz) diced cooked chicken

*Sauce*

50 g (2 oz) marge
50 g (2 oz) flour
500 ml (1 pint) milk
salt and pepper

Grease a large, preferably shallow casserole or baking dish and spread the drained spinach over the base. Make the sauce with the marge, flour, and milk, season well and mix in the rice and chicken. Pour the mixture over the layer of spinach, scatter the cheese to cover the whole top, and bake uncovered at 350°F (180°C or gas 4) for 30 minutes while somebody else lays the table and picks up the newspapers.

And that's a month's quota of main course recipes fair and square. It would be tedious to state at the end of each one its nourishment quota in terms of food values, but mothers think about these things and you might be sceptical, especially since a lot of the ingredients come out of tins. Don't worry: each and every one is stuffed with nutritious elements to make children the most successful kind of growth industry you've ever heard of. You'll find fresh vegetables in the next chapter, but pause here to remember never, never to tell the kids that anything is good for them.

# 3 Vegetables

A couple of popular half-truths tend to conceal the true facts about vegetables. One is that vegetables are vital to the health and strength of growing children; the other is that vegetables aren't all that vital, and children get the necessary vitamins from fruit and other foods anyway.

Three facts are somewhere in between. The first is that vegetables, especially green ones, are 'good' for kids because they contain valuable minerals and vitamin C. Second, children are notoriously difficult about eating them – probably because mothers get over-heated about their health values. And the third is that vegetables are no good to anyone, least of all to growing children, if they are *over-cooked*.

The way mums cook vegetables for children can establish a lifelong habit of happy veg eating. Or not. The traditional English way of cooking veg, for example, usually boils down to *boiling* them, fast and furiously, in far too much water for far too long. Some cooks start them off in *cold* water, cheerfully ensuring the maximum loss of flavour and vitamins. (Leaving prepared vegetables in cold water before cooking them has much the same effect.)

For most practical purposes the best way of cooking prepared veg is to put them straight into boiling salted water and *immediately pour most of the water off*. Then cover the pan with a tight-fitting lid and *simmer*, partly in water and partly in steam, over low heat for the bare minimum of time to make the stuff tender. For most young green vegetables 5 minutes is enough. Older and heftier veg like cabbage, celery, and cauliflower, will take a little longer; it's impossible to give accurate timings here, because everything depends on the type and age of the veg. As a general rule you should err on the short side. If you think the vegetable is under-cooked when you take off the lid and prod it, you can always simmer for a little longer or drain it and then add a nugget of butter or marge before cooking on for another couple of minutes.

A number of mums who take both veg and kids seriously insist that the only way to get it right is to use a *steamer*. This is a double-decker pan: the top pan has a perforated bottom to let steam through from boiling water in the lower pan. Steamers come in handy for heating up little dishes of left-overs, and when you're actually cooking vegetables there's no monkeying with boiling water before and after cooking. At the same time it is all too easy to leave food in the steamer for too long in the happy belief that if you turn off the heat the stuff will just stay hot. It will, but it will get over-cooked too.

A few conscientious mothers manage to persuade their children that *raw* vegetables are lovely. (It's certainly true that for best vitamin value most vegetables should be eaten raw, but not many mums are likely to get very far by pointing out to their kids how big and strong and healthy rabbits are.) The rest of us muddle along, handing out a raw carrot now and again and wishing our children would develop a liking for salads. Most do, eventually, but in the meantime mothers feel bound to produce some kind of vegetable some of the time. Cooking them properly is a fair start towards getting children to eat and like them.

It would be asking far too much to go all out on elaborate and expensive ways of cooking veg for children who, when the chips are down, are quite likely to wriggle out of eating them anyway. They merely merit a little care so that they'll taste better. *Braising*, for instance, is an easy, interesting, and under-used method (see page 39). Our chances of getting the children to eat vegetables improve spectacularly if we try to forget about their health properties and treat them like the mother who carefully cooked and ate a lot of spinach all by herself, refusing to give her kids so much as a mouthful. She loves spinach, that's all; and now her kids do too.

Here are some tried and proven ways with veg, some standard, some more interesting. We'll start with green and proceed through the other colours; and you'll find root vegetables and potatoes at the end.

**Peas**

Small fresh peas should be simmered for 5 minutes or less in a little boiling salted water. Then drain, add a teaspoon of sugar and a knob of butter and rattle the pan for a minute over the heat.

If frozen, and the packet says boil for 5 minutes, make it 4 (this goes for almost all frozen green veg).

Older peas are tough and will take longer. And if the children will swallow it they taste good with a little sliced cooked onion mixed in at the end.

A good pea purée can be made by mashing cooked peas with milk and butter or marge – very easy if you have a liquidizer. Taste for seasoning and stir in some chopped mint and a little black pepper if you think you can get away with it.

**Beans: broad**

There's a world of difference between little new broad beans and big tough elderly ones, which should be skinned to taste good. Simmer little new ones quickly in a little boiling water and shake them after draining, with a knob of butter or marge.

Old ones are better boiled in stock rather than water, and then mixed into a white sauce before serving. Use part-stock, part-milk for the sauce.

**Beans: haricot**

These are what the French call Haricots Verts and we call French beans; rounded green pods which, when allowed to mature, open up to provide those white dried beans we usually call butter beans.

Wash young pods first, if fresh, then simmer whole in a little boiling water under a tight lid for less than 10 minutes. They should be crunchy, not flabby – the kids can be allowed to eat them in their fingers.

Butter or dried beans should be soaked in cold water for 24 hours, then simmered in salted stock till tender.

**Beans: runner**

Wash these *before*, not after, you slice them. Cook as for peas, but leave out the sugar in the final minute, and substitute a little salt and pepper.

**Broccoli**

Cook fresh broccoli as you cook cauliflower (see page 41). If frozen, boil for a minute less than the packet directions demand and then toss for a final minute in butter and breadcrumbs. Some kids won't look at broccoli, but it rings a change.

**Brussels sprouts**

The watery mush of large, over-cooked sprouts is as far removed from the nutty taste of small, barely-cooked ones as mothers are from the Sea of Tranquillity. No wonder children fight them off; but sprouts are a readily available fresh vegetable throughout the winter and we'd be hard put to do without them. The smaller and more tight-leaved they are, the better – discard *all* loose outer leaves and try to keep them to a uniform size so they will cook evenly. If they're large, make two deep cuts across the stalk.

Simmer in a very little salted water for just over 5 minutes under a tight lid; then drain and toss in a knob of butter and a little seasoning. Serve them in a light gravy if all else fails.

**Cabbage**

Don't skip this. Cabbage needs no special pleading; properly cooked, it is delicious.

First, steel yourself not to cook it all; most cabbages are too big for one meal for four. Second, chop it small. Third, wash the bits in cold salty water and drain. Now put it straight into a pan over medium heat *without any water*. When it starts to steam, stir round and add a piece of butter or marge, then put on the lid and turn down the heat. Simmer for 10-15 minutes, then drain well – it makes a lot of juice on its own – and mix in a little more butter or some tasty meat dripping, along with some seasoning if necessary. *Cabbage should be crunchy, not slushy.*

You can mix cooked cabbage into a white sauce flavoured with as much mustard as you can get away with without the kids noticing; or serve it with frizzled pieces of bacon and a little top-of-the-milk mixed into it. (This makes a good supper dish.)

Or simmer it in a little stock, and serve in a parsley sauce made with the stock.

Or simmer it with some chopped onion in a savoury meat gravy – left-over gravy is fine.

However you serve cabbage, it's only fair not to dish out big helpings to children who may have a built-in resistance to it anyway. (If left-over cabbage threatens to take over the kitchen wall to wall, use it for flavouring in potato soup, which is what happens to left-over potatoes; boil up potatoes, cabbage and seasoning in a pint of milk (500 ml), then liquidize or sieve.)

**Leeks**

Leeks are inexpensive, much under-rated and horribly slimy if over-cooked – which is why they are under-rated.

Trim, wash well, then either chop rather fine or leave whole. Simmer briefly in a little salted boiling water or a mixture of stock and milk. Serve in a sauce or with bread-crumbs or both.

If leeks are chopped for children they are better cooked only in a knob of butter and their own juice. Five minutes should be long enough under the lid.

Or you can *braise* – a good way of cooking certain vegetables. The whole thing happens in one all-purpose casserole, like this: *To braise,* melt a piece of dripping, butter, or marge in a hot casserole or pan and fry some chopped onion golden brown. Add the prepared vegetable (leeks, celery, carrots, red cabbage) and shake round to coat with the fat. When everything is hot, but not dry, sprinkle in about a teaspoonful of flour and some salt and pepper, then stir in half-a-teacupful of water or stock. (Or less; leeks, for example, make their own liquid so don't overdo yours.) Bring to the boil, then cover tightly and continue cooking over very low heat or in a moderate oven for up to an hour. A drop or two of Worcestershire sauce added at the end tastes good, and a spoonful of cooking or left-over wine improves all braised vegetables. Serve as cooked, or with breadcrumbs on top.

**Spinach**

Some of us loathe spinach and always have; others love it and can't remember when they didn't. The same goes for kids. Maybe if we didn't push spinach into our babies so early they could come across it as a lovely surprise later. In any event spinach has a reputation both for instant health and as a troublemaker. It also has a distinctive taste which is either a winner or not. If you find yourself telling a child to eat his spinach so he'll have muscles like Popeye you can reckon you're on a loser. For the time being anyway.

Fresh spinach sounds like a lot of work, and it is, but it's the best. A huge basketful boils down to one small dishful – it shrinks as magically as the housekeeping money. Tear the leaves off the stalks, wash in cold water and drain. Now stuff the wet leaves into a pan over fairly high heat and shake in a very little salt. When it starts to bubble and steam, turn down the heat and cover with a tight lid while it simmers in steam and its own juice for between 5 and 10 minutes. Drain very thoroughly, then chop and return to the pan to heat through in a little melted butter. A white sauce mixed into it may help to sell it to a suspicious child. Better still, stir in some cream.

Leaf and puréed spinach come in tins and frozen packets and are much less effort. Puréed spinach in a sauce is often tolerated by children who won't eat leaf. In every case it's important to squeeze out *all* the liquid after cooking – evil pools of green water oozing over plates are enough to put anyone off.

**Beetroot**

Beetroot is usually sold ready-cooked, which is a pity because it's much nicer freshly boiled. Beets are a useful hot vegetable for children because they taste sweet and are a pretty colour far removed from the dreaded green. Kids who won't eat beets cold in a salad are often happy with beets hot in a white sauce; or chopped and tossed in butter and a little parsley. Small beets cooked at home are best. If you buy large cooked ones they should be skinned, sliced, and heated through in sauce or butter before serving.

**Carrots**

Carrots, like peas, are pretty popular. Both taste sweet, which helps. Small young carrots simmered whole and served with butter or a parsley sauce are delicate and delicious. Older ones are better sliced thinly and simmered in salted water or stock.

Big tough carrots should be cut lengthwise and *braised* (see page 39). If you cook them this way they will take about an hour in a moderate oven, 325-350°F (170-180°C or gas 3-4).

Carrots sliced into matchsticks, boiled for a few minutes and tossed in butter and breadcrumbs look and taste irresistible to all but the most confirmed vegetable-hater. They are a bother to do, but worth it.

### Cauliflower

Spanking white tight cauliflower is not always easy to come by, but if you get one it should be cooked within a day or so; cauliflower quickly goes stale. If yours looks sad and sorry, blanch it by pouring boiling water over it, then drain fast and cook in a little boiling water under a tight lid. The blanching won't help the food value but it will help the flavour.

Cauliflower in separated florets takes 15 minutes or so to cook, and can be served tossed in butter with fried stale breadcrumbs, or parsley; or in a white sauce flavoured with cheese or chopped egg. Don't mash it – it turns a nasty colour.

### Celery

Everything said about leeks can be said with equal emphasis about celery: both stand a better chance with children if we spare a minute to get the cooking right. You can boil celery or braise it, and it takes longer to cook than green veg; 15-20 minutes boiling or about an hour's braising is enough.

Older, stringy celery needs careful preparation if the kids are not to complain about thread-like tendrils tangling in their teeth. If they find the appearance of celery pallid and boring you can serve it in a white sauce spiked with food colouring.

And for all your trouble, a raw stick in a child's hand any old time is worth two cooked ones on the plate. If a chunk of cheese is in the other hand you can relax; the combination of cheese and celery packs a nourishing punch, besides being quite a favourite.

### Onions

Children who wouldn't look an onion in the eye have been known to eat onion rings battered and deep fried and then moan because mum didn't make enough. The fritter batter on page 60 is handy (leave out the sugar); here is an alternative.

Beat 50 g (2 oz) of plain flour and a pinch of salt with 4 tablespoons of tepid water and a dessertspoon of oil. Fold in a stiffly beaten egg white just before you start cooking. Coat onion rings in the mixture and deep fry in hot oil or lard until crisp and golden brown.

You can braise onions like celery, carrots, and leeks (see page 39); or bake them in their skins in the oven like jacket potatoes.

Onions are good boiled in milk and a bit of butter and served in a sauce made from the liquid; cooked onion has a subtle, sweet flavour very different from the raw tear-jerker.

Baby onions baked in the fat around a Sunday joint taste delicious, and they flavour the gravy as well.

## Red cabbage

Chop, wash and drain it like ordinary cabbage (page 38). Now braise it like leeks (see page 39), putting in a dessertspoon of sugar, another of wine vinegar and a drip of wine if you have any. Add a few raisins or sultanas to take the kids' minds off the fact that it's cabbage and it looks funny. It's a good veg.

## Tomatoes

Firm tomatoes which are not quite ripe are best for cooking. Bake whole; or bake them cut up with a chopped onion, a teaspoon of sugar, a knob of butter and some pepper and salt. A layer of breadcrumbs and grated cheese over this mixture turns it into a dish you could take anywhere.

It's worth saying that tomatoes are worth peeling for children. Prick each one and cover with boiling water for a minute, then dunk in cold water and drain. The skins will then slide off easily.

**Vegetable marrow**

This is best baked in the oven, uncovered, to concentrate the liquid it makes. It tends to be watery and can go mushy if you boil it.

Marrow stuffed with a meat mixture is good as a complete meal. Peel a marrow and lop off a slice lengthwise, leaving a boat-shaped piece filled with seeds and pith. Scrape all this out and fill the hollow with a mixture of mince flavoured with onion or parsley; then scatter breadcrumbs over the top and bake uncovered in the oven at 400°F (200°C or gas 6) for about an hour. Meanwhile the children can manufacture a mast and sail to stick into it just before serving, and if you're really keen you can make oars for the vessel out of raw celery sticks or strips of raw carrot.

Alternatively put the long slice back on top and tie the marrow round with string at either end before baking.

Courgettes (zucchini) look like baby marrows, but you don't need to peel these. Wipe them, then slice and fry in oil or butter for 5-10 minutes. A small can of tomatoes (or a few chopped fresh ones) stirred into fried courgettes makes a delicious vegetable dish.

**Parsnips**

Humble root vegetables often get the poor relation treatment – we know them but avoid them. It's unfair; poor relations can turn out to have hidden talents, besides being very nice indeed.

Parsnips should be peeled and cooked whole if they are small, otherwise slice them lengthwise to speed up the cooking time. Boil them for about the same time as you boil potatoes, in a little salted water, or milk-and-water, or stock, and use a saucepan with a tight lid. They cook to a potato-like consistency and have a sweet, slightly woody flavour.

Mash cooked parsnips with butter; or serve them whole in a white sauce made from the liquid they have been cooked in.

You can bake them in the fat around a joint, or separately in a covered casserole with a little butter and seasoning. This way they will take about 1-1½ hours in a moderate oven, 350°F (180°C or gas 4).

### Turnips and swedes

Turnips are small white globes ranging in size from ping-pong balls to cricket balls. Swedes are larger and coarser with a purply skin.

Peel and chop turnips and simmer them in stock, then serve in a sauce made from the liquid. Or mash them up with butter, seasoning, and parsley.

A swede should be peeled, chopped, and simmered in a little salted water and its own steam before mashing it with butter. You can also roast pieces of swede around a piece of meat, or braise them in the oven for about an hour.

Butter makes all the difference to root veg, and since they are less expensive than most other vegetables, we think they deserve the extravagance of butter along with them.

### Potatoes

If mothers are as sick as we are of all these good reasons for taking trouble with vegetables, here is a reason for taking no trouble with potatoes. Recent studies carried out on teeth in the British Isles came up with the finding that Irish children living in rural districts, where potatoes boiled in the skins form a major part of their diet, have better teeth than their urban counterparts. It seems there may be a direct connection between unpeeled potatoes and good teeth.

Don't take it as an insult if we offer some ways and means with spuds that you know in your sleep. In fact they are a difficult vegetable to cook well. A good greengrocer should be able to tell you what types are marketed in his area, and how they behave in the cooking.

### Baked jacket potatoes

Scrub, rinse, and dry. Now prick them with a fork and rub them over with a piece of buttery or oily paper. Sprinkle with salt and bake at 400°F (200°C or gas 6) for about an hour. Squeeze gently in a cloth and if the potato feels soft, it is ready. Prick again with the fork to let the steam escape and return to the oven for a minute or two – this makes the potato floury. The skins are very good eaten with extra butter.

## Boiled spuds

If you must peel, peel thinly, because the potato's prime food value lies directly under the skin. Put them in boiling water, pour away some of it, and then simmer the spuds under a tilted lid to let some of the steam escape. After about 15 minutes they should be just firm in the middle (test with a skewer or a sharp knife) and you can drain off the water and let them dry out over very low heat for a minute, shaking gently to prevent sticking.

Sprinkle with salt and a little chopped parsley, then add a piece of butter and serve. Bacon fat is good with potatoes boiled in their skins.

## Chips

Chips don't have to be chip-shaped; any kind of cut will do, and many a child believes solemnly that crinkly taste nicer than straight. Matchstick chips take longer to prepare but cook fast and are deliciously thin and crispy. Very thinly-sliced potato rounds can be as popular as crisps bought in a packet, besides being a lot cheaper.

Whatever cut they are, there's no need to cover chips completely with boiling fat. About 150 ml (6-7 fl oz) of oil or dripping is enough for a batch of chips for four. The important item is a large, deep, thick pan. Such pans are top-quality and top-price and top-priority for good chips and good deep-frying in general.

Heat up the fat while you cut the potatoes and dry them. When the fat has stopped bubbling, slide in the chips and *turn down the heat*. They should be cooked slowly at first, and then over increased heat for the last 5 or 10 minutes. Standard-sized chips will take 15-20 minutes and can be left to look after themselves, with a friendly shake now and again, until the final crisping.

When they're crisp outside and, hopefully, floury in the middle, lift out carefully and keep them hot on absorbent kitchen paper in a dish in a low oven.

### Creamy spuds

Peel and slice potatoes and shake them in seasoned flour. Lay them in overlapping layers in a greased casserole dish, then pour in milk until the slices are almost, but not quite, covered. Dot the top with bits of butter or marge and sprinkle on a little grated nutmeg.

Bake uncovered in the oven at 400°F (200°C or gas 6) for between 1 and 2 hours; spike with a skewer to see if the dish is done. The top should go brown, but if you think it is cooking too fast you should reduce the heat to 300°F (150°C or gas 2) and top up with a little more milk. Different types of potatoes take longer to cook – Majestics will take longer than King Edwards, for example. And don't worry about the nutmeg; the kids won't notice it and it gives the dish a good flavour.

### Mashed potatoes

Ideally, *use warm milk*. That means another pan to wash up, we know, but cold milk hardens the starch in potatoes and makes them go lumpy in the mashing. Mash in a piece of butter, a little salt and pepper and maybe some chopped onion, parsley, or chives.

Potatoes mashed with hotted-up gravy left over from a roast are very good with cold meat; you can cheer up the dark brown colour with sprigs of parsley.

### Roast potatoes

Bake these in the fat around a joint; or separately like this:

Heat up some dripping in a baking tin in a hot oven, 450°F (230°C or gas 8), while you peel and cut potatoes to an even size. Sprinkle them with seasoned flour and put them into the tin. After 10 minutes or so shake them around to coat them all over with the fat. They will take about an hour altogether to roast, and if you turn them over halfway through the cooking they will brown evenly.

An alternative and quicker way is to parboil potatoes for 10 minutes, then deep-fry for another 10.

### Sauté potatoes

A useful way of using up left-over spuds which have been boiled in their skins (don't skin them until just before you need them):

Peel off the skin, slice the potatoes and heat some dripping or marge in a frying pan while you chop a little onion and parsley. Fry the whole lot together, shaking them around, and serve very hot. The less fat you use, the browner and crisper they will be, but young children tend to like them soft and just coloured.

### And finally, new potatoes

In a perfect world every mum would have her own little garden and grow her own. As things are, we heard recently that in some parts of the country allotments were going begging. There can be no better way of using an allotment, even a window box, than for growing potatoes.

The smallest, newest spuds should be lightly scraped, *not* peeled, then dropped into boiling salted water with a little mint (if you have room for it in that window box). Simmer for a few minutes, then drain, allow to dry, and serve with butter, seasoning, and chopped parsley.

Alternatively, skip the water and toss them in melted butter over the heat for a few minutes before putting them in a baking tin and grilling them until they are brown and crisp.

Slightly older, larger new potatoes are good sliced and cooked only in butter and their own steam.

There are, of course, lots of other ways of dealing with potatoes; but only one more we can usefully recommend. We do so with feeling.

Take a selection of the poorly-flavoured, poorly-textured

varieties of potato so readily available to us all, and place them in a cardboard box – a shoe box, say. Now write a letter of complaint and put that in the box with the potatoes. Finally wrap the box in brown paper, tie it securely with string, and post the parcel to the Potato Marketing Board.

# 4 Puddings

The promise of a splendid pudding will often lead a reluctant child through meat-and-veg where all other blandishments fail (see Chapter 7 page 128 for bribes and bribery). Kids love the idea of pudding – almost any old pudding – and there is seldom any need to gild the lily and make them even more enjoyable by lashing out with heart, soul, and cream.

Enjoyment aside, puddings can be too much of a good thing; we're sure that it is both better and less trouble in the long run to concentrate on making the main course a winner. The whole sticky business of sweets and sweet things is dealt with in the Problems chapter, but it is reasonable to anticipate it here. Children need carbohydrates just as they need proteins and vitamins and iron and love, but they don't need carbohydrates in anything like the amounts pushed at them from babyhood in countless well-meaning families. This applies to puddings as much as to actual candy. You may fear that your skinny ten-year-old will fade into thin air if he doesn't get his pudding, but in fact he will do nothing of the kind if he's eating normally in every other way. He will merely remark bitterly that every other mother in the world, especially his best friend's mother, makes puddings and you (withering scorn) don't. He will also probably have better teeth, better skin, and a better chance of reaching middle age without being overweight. Wanting sweet things is normal, because the inner man wants a balanced diet and carbohydrates form part of the balance. But it is too easy and too common to establish the habit of wanting more sweet things than we need. Maybe sweet things are associated in mothers' minds with feelings of comfort or reward from our own childhood. (Very likely, and that's one reason why it's so hard to diet.)

One mother we know swears that, so help her, she makes no more than a dozen puddings a year. Her children get fruit, nuts, raisins, yoghurt or nothing after the meat-and-veg. She'll make a jelly now and again, but when she makes pudding it's with adults in mind. She says that she didn't start this regime until she got teeth-conscious with her eldest's 6-year-old molars, so she had a habit to break; but it worked out a lot easier than she thought it would. It's a policy of perfection, but it shows – the kids are flourishing and she's slim at last.

Be that as it may, policies of perfection are tiresome and puddings can be a pleasure and a joy. They are also a good way of getting children to eat eggs and milk if they're tricky over these. Most of the best puddings for children are easy and quick and a lot don't need any cooking at all. The number of instant mixes on the market, for example, would keep you in puddings for weeks if the housekeeping and the kids could stand it. Many children could, and cheerfully, but we'd rather have ice-cream than instant mix. It's a wise mother who always has some ice-cream by her, if only as a face-saver. When healthful fruit crumble isn't going well we can always pretend we meant to have ice-cream. (This is what is known as peace with honour: the fruit crumble can be trotted out with custard at supper time and maybe we should have stuck to ice-cream in the first place.) Here is a selection of sauces to jazz up ice-cream for those of us who feel guilty about lovely old ice-cream making life so simple so often.

## The top ten

*Chocolate peppermint:* Melt 10 choc mints with 3 tablespoons top-of-the-milk, or single cream, in a bowl over simmering water. When they soften, stir until smooth.

*Crunchie:* Melt 50 g (2 oz) butter with 2 tablespoons golden syrup. When it boils, add a squeeze of lemon juice and boil again for half a minute, then quickly mix in about 12 tablespoons of cornflakes.

*Fudge:* Melt 100 g (4 oz) fudge with 1-2 tablespoons of milk, or evaporated milk, in a bowl over hot water.

*Mellow-Mallow:* Heat 100 g (¼ lb) marshmallows with 25 g (1 oz) plain chocolate in 2 tablespoons of milk. Stir until the mallows melt and the mixture thickens, then remove from the heat and stir in 1 level teaspoon ground ginger and another tablespoon of milk.

*Butterscotch:* Heat gently 50 g (2 oz) brown sugar, 25 g (1 oz) butter and a tablespoonful golden syrup until the sugar dissolves. Boil steadily for 5 minutes, then add 2 tablespoonfuls of water and boil it up again, stirring well.

*Tutti-Frutti:* Heat a tin of pie filling (apricot is good) and pour it over the ice-cream.

*It's-A-Honey:* Melt 4 tablespoons of honey, pour over ice-cream and top with chopped nuts.

*'s Marvellous:* Melt a Mars Bar (or any toffee bar covered with chocolate) in a bowl over hot water, with a tablespoon or two of milk to help it dissolve.

*Jam Crunch:* Melt 4 tablespoonfuls of jam and stir in a tablespoonful of crumbled biscuits. (Cherry jam with crushed digestive biscuits is good.)

*Chocolate Surprise:* So-called because you and the kids will be as surprised as we are to find that we can make chocolate sauce almost as easily as getting it out of the tube or tin. Melt together 100 g (4 oz) plain dark chocolate, 12 g (½ oz) butter and 1-2 tablespoons of water or coffee in a bowl over hot water.

If you skip to the end of this chapter you'll find a couple of recipes for home-made ice-cream that are so easy and so good, you'll wonder why you ever bought the stuff ready-made (don't wonder too hard).

This first batch of real puddings mostly use milk, either fresh or evaporated, and quite a few of them use eggs too. If you can remember always to keep a tin of evaporated milk in the refrigerator you will save a lot of effort and cash. It will whip like cream if it's cold, but *only* if it's cold.

**One minute mousse**

1 large tin chilled evaporated milk
1 tin pie-filling (cherry is good) or some cooked fruit

Whip the milk semi-stiff, fold in the pie-filling or fruit, pour into bowl or bowls. Bingo.

**Minute mousse mark II**

1 packet instant milk pudding powder
enough fresh milk to make up the packet as directed
1 small tin chilled evaporated milk

Make up the instant pudding, whip the evaporated milk and fold in. Decorate with sugar strands or grated chocolate if you feel an urgent need to make the gesture.

**Mighty mousse**

1 packet of jelly
500 g (1 lb) fresh fruit or a large tin (440 g or 16 oz) fruit in syrup
1 large tin chilled evaporated milk
125 ml (5 fl oz or ¼ pint) water *or* the juice drained from a tin of fruit

Melt the jelly in boiling water or boiling drained fruit juice and leave until nearly setting. Then whisk the milk stiff, whisk in the jelly mixture and finally fold in the fruit. Chill till set.

## Chocolate mousse minor

There's a major chocolate mousse which is more impressive than this one (page 64), but if you keep it for special occasions the kids can be pacified now. Now is what counts.

50 g (2 oz) drinking chocolate powder
1½ level dessertspoons sugar
1 packet gelatine (½ oz or 10 g)
3 tablespoons water
1 small tin chilled evaporated milk

Dissolve the chocolate, sugar, and gelatine in the water over low heat, and don't get the mixture too hot because now you have to hang around to let it get cool. Whip the evaporated milk and whisk in the mixture a little at a time. (You can use powdered coffee for this if the kids like it.)

## Fruit cream

500 g (1 lb) any stewed fresh fruit or a large tin (822 g, 1 lb 13 oz) of drained fruit
2 tablespoonfuls sugar
packet gelatine (10 g or ½ oz)
half a large tin chilled evaporated milk, or 1 small tin

Mash, sieve, or liquidize the fruit and whip the milk fairly stiff. Dissolve the gelatine in 3 tablespoonfuls of water (or some of the drained juice from the tin) and whisk it into the milk. Now add the fruit purée and sugar to taste.

It cheers up a pallid, rather nondescript pudding to stir in a drop or two of food colouring, and you can do that here – red or yellow or green, like the traffic lights. Pour into a rinsed mould or loaf tin and leave to set. Unmould by dipping the base into hot water and turning the pudding on to a plate. Decorate with a few little coloured sweets.

The next half-dozen recipes all use fresh milk and children have been eating versions of them for generations. That's why mums think they're boring. They're not; but the old-fashioned mothers and nannies who served them up every single day probably were.

**Queen of puddings**

500 ml (1 pint) milk
50 g (2 oz) marge or butter
a squeeze of lemon juice
a pinch of salt
100 g (4 oz) breadcrumbs
2 separated eggs
2 tablespoonfuls jam (any kind)
2 tablespoonfuls sugar

Bring the milk, marge, lemon juice, salt, and crumbs slowly to the boil. Simmer for a few minutes while you beat up the egg yolks and stir them into the mixture. Now pour it into a casserole and bake in a medium oven, 350°F (180°C or gas 4) for 20-30 minutes. Take it out and let it cool a little while you beat the egg whites stiffly and fold in the sugar. Spread the jam over the top of the pudding, cover with the meringue and bake again for about 20 minutes. This is a marvellous but rather complicated pudding, so mothers who make it should be Queen for the Day.

**Never-fail custard sauce**

This is where you're going to get eggs and milk into the kids by the gallon if you want to. Start with the sauce. Children like custard sauce on almost anything (we know a mother who puts it on green vegetables – why not?). Instant custard powder mixed and cooked with milk is easiest and cheapest; but if eggs are what interest you, take it from here.

375 ml (¾ pint) milk
2 egg yolks
1 tablespoon sugar
1 teaspoon custard powder

While the milk is warming, beat up the egg yolks and sugar in a bowl and blend in the custard powder. Now pour the warm milk on to the paste and stir well. Return the mixture to the milk pan and cook gently, stirring, until the mixture just coats the back of the spoon you're stirring it with. If the tell-tale pale yellow of real custard alerts your children to the presence of real egg, make it bright yellow with food colouring and put the custard powder tin on the table without a word.

The left-over egg whites make a good meringue topping

for a dull pudding – or have a look at Baked Alaska (page 68) and Pavlova (page 69).

**Carry-on custard**

Here's the basic recipe; you carry on from there to ring the changes, either by coating the bottom of the dish with crumbled biscuits, or caramel (below); try mixing in some lemon rind, or orange rind, or grated coconut; or stirring in 25 g (1 oz) of cocoa or coffee powder, or a drop or two of vanilla essence, or anything else you can think up.

375 ml (¾ pint) milk
3 whole big eggs or 4 egg yolks
25 g (1 oz) sugar
any kind of appropriate flavouring
any kind of decoration

Beat the eggs and sugar together with the flavouring and pour in hot, not boiling milk. Now pour into a greased pie dish or casserole and stand this in a baking tin of cold water. Bake for at least 1½ hours in a slow oven, 275°F (140°C or gas 1 or 2), until firm. Ovens vary as much as egg custards, so the actual timing must be your own.

To steam, put the dish over very hot water and cook steadily for about the same length of time. Don't let the water boil, or the mixture will curdle. Curdled custard is not much fun.

**Caramel custard**

Heat together 3 tablespoonfuls of sugar and 3 tablespoonfuls of water with a squeeze of lemon juice, stirring all the time. When the mixture comes to the boil stop stirring and simmer until it is a rich brown. Pour this quickly over the base of your dish and swish it around to coat the sides. Pour your Carry-on custard mixture on top of this and steam or bake as before.

**Crispy rice pudding**

When you rush your plain rice pudding and your plain meat stew into your plain slow oven and set sail for the winter sales, this pudding can be turned into a better bargain when you get home after spending more than you reckoned to.

50-75 g (2-3 oz) pudding rice (round grain type)
500 ml (1 pint) milk
50 g (2 oz) sugar
a few raisins or sultanas

*Topping*

25 g (1 oz) brown sugar
25 g (1 oz) breadcrumbs
25 g (1 oz) melted butter

Wash the rice and put it in a greased pie dish or casserole with the sugar and milk. Add a knob of butter or suet to make it extra creamy, put the dish in a slow oven, 275°F (140°C or gas 1), and go to town for 2-3 hours. When you get back sprinkle the top with the brown sugar, crumbs, and melted butter and grill until crisp and golden.

## Creamy lemon rice

500 ml (1 pint) milk
75 g (3 oz) pudding rice
75 g (3 oz) sugar
2 separated eggs
the juice of ½ a lemon
some grated lemon rind

Bring the milk to the boil, then stir in the rice, re-boil, and simmer very gently for 30-45 minutes until the rice is very soft. Take off the heat and mix in the sugar, then the egg yolks one at a time, then the lemon juice and grated rind (don't over-do the lemon). Leave until cold, then beat the egg whites stiff and fold them into the mixture. Spoon into a serving dish and chill, if there's time.

## Peekaboo pears

4 fairly firm pears
4 teaspoons apricot jam
50 g (2 oz) pudding rice
500 ml (1 pint) milk
sugar to taste
1 small knob of butter (optional)

Peel and halve the pears and scoop out the cores. (Apples will do just as well, but you should cook for a little longer.) Fill each centre with a teaspoon of jam, then place them filled-side-down in a casserole. Heat the rice, milk, sugar, and butter together in a saucepan until the mixture starts to thicken, then pour it over the fruit. Bake slow in a oven, 300°F (150°C or gas 2) for an hour.

Young children tend to prefer lighter, milky puddings and sometimes turn up their noses at more substantial pies, flans, and sponges. But somewhere around the age of eight or nine, and thereafter for ten years, an increasing demand for solid stuff forces mothers into a long stint of stodge.

The next few recipes are *bases*, for flans and tarts; and *batters*, for pancakes and fritters; both of which catch up with us sooner or later. They don't fall into the really heavyweight pudding category, but they cope with a craving for calories and you can put healthy fruit, custards, and other confections inside them.

The first three make good, quick bases. Keep them in their dishes and don't try to turn them out. When you want a free-standing flan, use the shortcrust recipe on page 58.

**Biscuit base**

100 g (4 oz) butter or marge
25 g (1 oz) sugar (brown sugar gives a nicer flavour)
200 g (7 oz) crushed digestive biscuits

Melt the marge with the sugar and stir in the crushed biscuits. Press this mixture flat over the base and sides of a flan tin (or large plate, if you don't mind a flan without sides). It hardens as it cools, and then you can put in a filling. Use sweet biscuits for this base when you have a disreputable accumulation of broken bits and crumbs at the bottom of the biscuit tin, but leave out the sugar. Likewise leave it out if you're using chocolate-covered digestive biscuits.

**Rice crispie base** – gooey

125 g (5 oz) butter or marge
25 g (1 oz) sugar
100 g (4 oz) rice crispies

Proceed as for Biscuit base.

**Cornflake base** – crunchy

100 g (4 oz) butter or marge
50 g (2 oz) sugar
100 g (4 oz) crushed cornflakes

Cream the butter and sugar together, add the cornflakes and mix well. Now press it into a flan tin and chill before use.

**Shortcrust pastry base** – for sweet and savoury flans

100 g (4 oz) sifted flour
50 g (2 oz) marge, butter or a blend of either of these with lard
a pinch of salt
25 ml (1 fl oz) cold water – or less

Sift the flour and salt together, then cut the marge into it and rub into the flour until the mixture looks like fine breadcrumbs. Add only as much water as you need to bind the pastry together into a lump. It should be soft, not sticky. Roll out on a floured surface and line a flan tin.

Now you're going to bake it 'blind'. Prick the base all over with a fork and press in a circle of greaseproof paper the same size as the flan tin. Scatter in a handful of dried peas or beans or macaroni (keep a supply in a jar for this) and bake the flan in a hot oven, 325°F (170°C or gas 3), for 15 minutes. Whip out the beans and paper and return the flan to the oven for another 10 minutes to crisp the base. Now take out and cool before filling.

The catch about cooking with any kind of batter is that mum finds herself shackled to the stove throughout the cooking process while the kids pick that time to go on the rampage. Every expert tells us smugly that pancakes, fritters, and anything deep-fried should be eaten hot and fresh out of the pan; but life is different outside the pages of cookery books and mothers know it better than anybody. You can cook pancakes in advance if you stack them between layers of greaseproof paper, than wrap in a loose foil parcel which can be gently reheated in a low oven. Fritters and deep-fries are less co-operative and go soggy at the drop of an egg whisk; but if you drain them well and carefully on absorbent kitchen paper they will keep hot and fairly fresh in a partly-covered dish in a low oven for up to half-an-hour.

There are two keys to success when making fritters: roll your ingredients thoroughly in flour before battering; and make sure the fat is really hot to set the batter quickly. You should then lower the heat for the rest of the cooking. It all sounds like a lot of fuss and bother and tired feet, but pancakes and fritters are high on the popularity list, and now and then it's gratifying to hear the children say 'Got any more, mum?' or even 'Hey, thanks!'.

### Pancake batter

100 g (4 oz) plain flour
a pinch of salt
1 egg
250 ml (½ pint) milk
25 g (1 oz) melted butter or marge

Sift the flour and salt into a bowl and make a well in the middle. Break the egg into the well and beat in the flour, adding the milk a little at a time as you go along. If it goes lumpy, whisk like mad, but you can avoid lumps if you beat in the flour gradually. You can let it stand for an hour or so before cooking, but it's not vital. Stir in the melted butter or marge just before you start cooking, and if you're doubtful about the consistency add a little cold water. Pancake batter should be thin, like single cream. Thick pancakes are awful.

Now get out a frying pan – a small round one is ideal – and heat up a tablespoonful of oil in it. As faint smoke begins to rise, pour off the oil and turn down the heat. You're ready to go.

A puddle of batter in the kitchen ladle is enough to keep the pancake elegantly thin, but adequately round. Pour the batter into the pan, swirl it around to cover the base, and cook until the top bubbles. Now slide a palette knife underneath and flip it over, shaking the pan to bring it back into the middle. Cook the reverse side for another minute, then lay the pancake between pieces of greaseproof paper; pour another puddle of batter into the pan and start again. The oily pan, along with the melted butter in the batter, should mean that you don't have to add any more fat between pancakes, but we can't guarantee it. We do guarantee the pancakes' popularity rating with children from eight to eighty.

*Sweet pancake fillings*

The fillings are up to you: sugar and lemon juice, fruit purée like apple sauce with cinnamon, or jam, are all good. If you move with the speed of light you can even fill them with dollops of ice-cream, roll up, and coat with hot chocolate sauce.

**Fritter batter**

This one is thicker, because it has to stick to food. Self-raising flour (or plain flour with baking powder) should be used, but you can use plain for dusting the food *before* battering.

100 g (4 oz) self-raising flour (or plain, with 1 level teaspoon baking powder)
a pinch of salt
1 teaspoon sugar (leave this out for savouries)
1 egg
125 ml (5 fl oz or ¼ pint) milk

Mix the flour, salt, sugar, and egg together and stir in the milk gradually, beating out any lumps. Now it's ready, and it can stand around for a while until you are; or keep in the refrigerator for a day or so. Use it to coat floured apple rings, halved bananas, pineapple slices; or pieces of fish or chicken.

To cook, heat enough fat or oil in a frying pan to cover, and deep-fry. Cook quickly at a high temperature for a minute on each side, then lower the heat and cook more slowly – 5 minutes each side for apples, for example.

Stewed fruit is, ever and always, useful stuff to have around for any meal. And children can get very sick of it: they learn early that it's easy for mothers and good for them, and kick up trouble accordingly. Apart from dressing it up with custard or cream, a variety of toppings can be used to cloak the dreaded vitamin C, besides spinning out a small quantity of fruit and filling up the inner demand for stodge. All these toppings can be used with fresh stewed fruit or tinned fruit.

## Crumble toppings

We have two: a basic and a special. *Basic* consists of 150 g (6 oz) flour, 75 g (3 oz) marge, and a heaped teaspoon of sugar rubbed together and then baked on top of fruit, for about 30 minutes at 350°F (180°C or gas 4). *Special* is:

## Candy crumble

100 g (4 oz) plain flour
100 g (4 oz) marge
250 g (8 oz) sugar (white or brown)
1 teaspoon powdered cinnamon

Rub together all the ingredients to a crumbly texture and bake on top of unsweetened stewed apples at 350°F (180°C or gas 4) for 30 minutes.

## Sponge topping

2 eggs
50 g (2 oz) sugar
35 g (1½ oz) sifted plain flour

Beat the eggs and sugar till creamy, then fold in the sifted flour. Pour this over fruit and bake at 350°C (180°C or gas 4) for about 40 minutes.

## Cobbler topping

Fruit cobbler is very like fruit pie; the mixture used on top is easier than pastry and rather more interesting to look at.

25 g (1 oz) marge
100 g (4 oz) self-raising flour (or plain, with 1 level teaspoon baking powder)
50 g (2 oz) sugar
milk to mix

Rub the marge into the flour and add the sugar. Now mix to a fairly soft dough with a little milk, roll out on a floured board to about ½ in. thick, then cut out 2 in. rounds or triangles. Arrange these on top of cooked or tinned fruit and bake fast for 15 minutes in a hot oven, 450°F (230°C or gas 8).

## Crunchy cobbler

A fancier version of cobbler topping, much liked by ravenous teenagers and guaranteed to send their mothers staggering from the table to look up calorie charts.

250 g (8 oz) self-raising flour
a pinch of salt
50 g (2 oz) marge
water to mix
25 g (1 oz) softened butter or marge
50 g (2 oz) brown sugar

Sift the flour and salt, rub in the fat and mix to a soft dough with a little cold water. Roll out on a floury board to a rectangle about ¼ in. thick. Spread this with the softened butter, sprinkle on the brown sugar and roll it up like a Swiss roll. Cut the roll into thin slices, arrange these on top of your stewed or tinned fruit and bake in a hot oven, 425°F (220°C or gas 7), for about 20 minutes, until well risen and golden brown. If you dish this pudding up with cream or custard you'll deserve your reputation as the mother teenagers flock to from far and wide.

Now for a few real heavyweights. If painful memories of these puddings still haunt your dreams, and if you know your children are getting them at school anyway, pass on. We find, though, that for every mother who shudders at the recollection there is a father who goes misty-eyed with nostalgia when presented with a slice of stodge, joyfully hailed as 'Dead Man's Leg' and precipitating a flood of stories about football teams and whatever-happened-to-old-Stinker. (Old Stinker probably ate everybody under the table, went on into the insurance business and today tips the scales at 20 stone.) These puddings are splendid for adolescent boys who burn up energy in direct ratio to their mothers burning up the housekeeping money, but that's as far as they go. Don't let them get a grip for life.

**Apple brown Betty**

100 g (4 oz) brown breadcrumbs
500 g (1 lb) peeled and sliced cooking apples
50 g (2 oz) dried fruit
½ teaspoon mixed spice
25 g (1 oz) sugar
50 g (2 oz) marge
1 tablespoon golden syrup
2 teaspoons water

Grease a pudding basin and sprinkle some of the crumbs around the inside. Fill the basin with alternate layers of apples, dried fruit, breadcrumbs, spice, and sugar, ending with crumbs on top. Dab on the marge in little pieces and then mix the syrup with the water and pour over the pudding. Steam for 1½-2 hours.

### Roly poly pudding

250 g (8 oz) self-raising flour (or plain with 2 level teaspoons baking powder)
a pinch of salt
75-100 g (3-4 oz)) finely shredded suet
water to mix
150-250 g (6-8 oz) jam

Sift the flour and salt and mix in the suet. Mix to a rolling consistency with cold water and roll out on a floured board to about ¼ in. thick. Cut into a neat oblong, then spread with the jam, being careful not to take the jam right to the edges. Now turn in the side edges and roll up like a Swiss roll. Wrap lightly in greased greaseproof paper, then in a floured cloth, and steam for 2½ hours over boiling water. Make the kids chew hard; we get indigestion just looking at the recipe.

### Marmalade pudding

100 g (4 oz) self-raising flour (or plain, with 2 level teaspoons baking powder)
50 g (2 oz) suet or margarine
50 g (2 oz) breadcrumbs
50 g (2 oz) sugar
2 tablespoons marmalade
milk to mix

Sift the flour, then add the suet or rub in the marge. Stir in the breadcrumbs and sugar, then mix in the marmalade and enough milk to make it sticky. Put this into a greased basin, filling it no more than two-thirds full, as it will rise during cooking. Cover the basin carefully with greased greaseproof paper, foil, or a pudding cloth, tuck the edges down firmly, and steam over boiling water for 2½ hours. Serve with custard and/or dollops of marmalade.

### Crispy orange sponge

75 g (3 oz) butter
75 g (3 oz) brown sugar
75 g (3 oz) self-raising flour
1 egg
the juice and rind of 1 orange
25 g (1 oz) sugar, preferably caster

Melt the butter and stir in the brown sugar. Beat the eggs and stir them into the mixture with the flour. Turn into a small, square, greased baking tin and bake for about 15 minutes at 375°F (190°C or gas 5). In the meantime grate a tablespoonful or so of orange rind into a bowl. Squeeze out the orange juice, mix in the caster sugar and rind and spread this thin paste over the sponge as it comes from the oven. The juice sinks in and the top stays crispy, and this is a good pud.

The rest of this chapter might be called Puddings Plus. None of them are in the least difficult – no spun sugar or anything like that – but some of them involve cream and all of them are bad for your waistline and ours too. These are the puddings that boost morale, demonstrate love and good intentions, and cause squabbles over which child is going to scrape the bowl. If you make them just now and again the kids might learn a little appreciation, and they're worth a try because they're all good.

**Chocolate mousse major**

100 g (4 oz) plain dark chocolate
4 teaspoons water (or coffee, or brandy)
4 separated eggs

Melt the chocolate with the liquid in a bowl over hot water while you beat the egg yolks lightly. When the chocolate mixture has melted and cooled a little, beat the yolks in well and cool again. Now beat the egg whites stiff and fold them in. Pile the pudding in a pretty dish or individual glasses.

**Lemon mousse**

3 large separated eggs
2 or 3 lemons
100-250 g (4-8 oz) caster sugar (the amount depends on your kids' tastebuds, but try not to make it too sweet)
packet of gelatine (10 g or ½ oz)
3 tablespoons water

Separate the eggs and put the yolks in a large bowl with the sugar. Grate the rind of the lemons, beat this into the eggs and sugar and whisk the mixture until light and creamy. Gradually beat in squeezed lemon juice too. Dissolve the gelatine in the water (see Chapter 2 page 27) and stir into the mixture; and finally beat the egg whites and fold them in before pouring the pudding into a dish and leaving to set. (If the children have spat out rind before now, leave this out; strain the lemon mixture before folding in the egg whites.)

### Orange and apricot cream

This takes not only double cream but also, preferably, an electric blender to pulp the fruit. You could sieve the fruit, but it's tedious and we wouldn't want to do it every day. This pudding is too good for every day anyway.

1 orange
1 tin apricots (440 g or 15 oz)
1 medium-size carton (125 ml or 5 fl oz) double cream
sugar to taste

Wash the orange, slice it with the skin on, and take out the pips. Put the orange slices in a pan with the apricots and their syrup and simmer, covered, for 20 minutes, stirring now and again to prevent the fruit sticking. Now take it off the heat and strain excess juice into a jug. Blend or sieve the fruit mixture to a smooth paste, allow it to cool and stir in some juice to make it the consistency of thick cream. Add sugar to taste, whip the double cream lightly and fold it in. Chill, preferably overnight, in the fridge.

### Marshmallow mousse

1 tin (440 g or 15 oz) raspberries or strawberries, or 375 g (¾ lb) fresh or frozen
150 g (6 oz) marshmallows
1 small tin chilled evaporated milk
3 teaspoons lemon juice

Drain the fruit and melt the marshmallows in the juice over low heat. If you're using fresh fruit, melt the mallows in 125 ml (5 fl oz or ¼ pint) of milk and add a little extra sugar. Whip the evaporated milk stiff. When the mallow mixture is cool, beat in the whipped milk with the lemon juice. Now fold in the fruit, pile the pudding in a dish and chill.

**Fruit fool**

Only rich fools use cream to make fools; kids are happy with custard and so are we. If you feel you must have cream, serve it separately so it *shows*.

250 ml (½ pint) fruit purée (sieved or blended stewed apples, apricots, blackcurrants, gooseberries, rhubarb, raspberries, blackberries, etc)
250 ml (½ pint) custard (instant or egg: see page 54)
sugar to taste

Fold the ingredients together and pile in a dish. Serve with sponge fingers, or wafers, or biscuits, or just all alone. All alone is dull.

**Trad trifle**

Ye Olde Englishe Trifle is one of the mysteries of the British way of life. Other countries regard it with the respect usually accorded to the Mother of Parliaments; French chefs have been known to spend hours attempting it only to break into sobs. It's all nonsense, of course, but there's something about trifle that reflects the British genius for compromise: it tries to please most of the people most of the time. Aristocratic trifles have sherry and whisky and cream galore and we'll forget about those in favour of the democratic majority. This version is for the child-on-the-Clapham-omnibus.

1 orange jelly
1 small tin mandarin oranges
1 packet trifle sponges (or sponge fingers, or left-over sponge cake)
2 bananas
1 small tin chilled evaporated milk

Melt the jelly in a scant 250 ml (½ pint) of boiling water. Add the mandarin juice and enough water to bring it up to 375 ml (¾ pint). Arrange the sponges, mandarin pieces, and sliced bananas artistically in a dish and when the jelly liquid is cold pour it in. Allow to set, then whip the evaporated milk and pour it over the top.

### Toddlers' trifle

This is for that early phase of childhood when kids want to know what *is* it, not what's in it. You can cry 'trifle' with a clear conscience, and they may begin to learn that one word can have a multitude of meanings. (Like 'British'.)

1 raspberry Swiss roll
1 small tin raspberries (or equivalent fresh or frozen)
1 egg white
2 teaspoons caster sugar

Line a lightly greased ovenproof dish with the sliced Swiss roll. Empty the raspberries over the top (if fresh, don't add any liquid, the fruit makes its own juice). Now whip the egg white stiff, fold in one teaspoon of the sugar and cover the fruit with the meringue mixture. Sprinkle with the rest of the sugar and bake at 325°F (170°C or gas 3) for half an hour. There'll be an egg yolk floating around the kitchen now, so make a custard sauce (see page 54) to use later before you lose track of it. Wasting egg *hurts*.

*Caramelizing* sounds difficult and dangerous and the kind of thing you read about in glossy cookbooks with 'creme brulée' confidently leading the puddings. In fact it's as easy as grilling brown sugar for 2 minutes, and that's exactly what it is. Any fruit, flattened off with a layer of cream or custard and well chilled can be caramelized; so can any chilled egg custard. All you do is set the grill fast and hot, sprinkle just under ¼ in. of soft brown or caster sugar over the pudding (make sure the layer goes right to the edge all round) and flash the dish under the hot grill for 2 minutes. It bubbles and heaves and turns glassy brown. (Be sure to use an ovenproof dish, and if the grill is really hot, 2 minutes should be enough – over-cooked caramel is tough.) The sound of crunching will be broken only by the screech of the child whose wiggly tooth has finally come out under stress. Two warnings: don't, whatever you do, be tempted to touch the caramel topping until you're sure it's cool; and don't, please, try it out on grandparents who may be privately adjusting to false teeth.

## Grape crunch

500 g (1 lb) white grapes (the small seedless ones are ideal, and don't waste effort peeling them unless the skins are very tough)
3 tablespoons sherry (optional)
250 ml ($\frac{1}{2}$ pint) custard (or a large carton double cream, whipped)
enough moist brown sugar for the caramel topping (perhaps 10 tablespoons)

Wash the grapes and pip if necessary. Put them in an ovenproof dish, leaving a clear 1 cm ($\frac{1}{2}$ in.) at the top. Trickle in the sherry if you like, then whip the cream and smooth it over the top of the fruit. (Similarly if you're using custard.) Chill for at least 3 hours, then heat up the grill, spread your layer of brown sugar over the pudding and caramelize. You can do this with sliced oranges, or cooked apple slices, or any drained tin of fruit; and it turns plain old baked egg custard (Carry-on custard page 55) into a party pudding in 2 minutes flat. And like we said, *don't touch it till it cools.*

## Baked Alaska

This recipe and the next one are classic puddings and like all classics they're surrounded by a mist of mystique, in these two cases wholly undeserved. They're both easy, they're both quick, and they both use up left-over egg whites in the nicest possible way. Ditch your prejudices and remember this is a cookbook for mothers cooking for children. We're not out to make problems for you. (If left-over yolks, not whites, are your problem, go back to the custards on pages 54 and 55.)

3-5 egg whites
3-5 tablespoons (100-150 g or 4-6 oz) sugar
1 Swiss roll
1 family-sized brick of ice-cream, chilled rock hard

Heat the oven to 450°F (230°C or gas 8) before you begin. Whisk the egg whites stiff and fold in an equivalent number of tablespoons of sugar. Slice the Swiss roll into rounds 1 cm ($\frac{1}{2}$ in.) thick and arrange them on an ovenproof dish. Now dump the block of ice-cream on top of the cake and smear the meringue mixture all over, sealing the edges carefully.

Bake for about 7 minutes in the hot oven and eat at once while the meringue is hot and crisp and the ice-cream cold and firm. So far as timing goes, we reckon to put the dish in the oven at the moment when the children are half-way through the main course and starting to whine about finishing it up. If they whine and pick at their plates for 4 minutes, you've got 3 left to clear the deck and serve the pudding.

**Pavlova**

3 egg whites
a pinch of salt
3 tablespoons sugar
another 3 tablespoons sugar mixed with 1 teaspoon cornflour
1 teaspoon vinegar

It helps a lot if you have a 20 cm (8 in.) cake tin with a detachable base. If you haven't got one you can make the meringue shell on a 20 cm (8 in.) circle drawn on greased greaseproof paper and laid on an ovenproof plate. Either way, keep the sides high and the centre hollowed out.

Grease the cake tin and line it with lightly greased greaseproof paper (or draw your circle on greased greaseproof paper and place it on a fireproof plate). Beat the egg whites with the pinch of salt till stiff, beat in 3 tablespoonfuls of sugar, then gently fold in the sugar-and-cornflour. Lastly mix in the vinegar. Pour the meringue mixture into the cake tin and make a hollow in the centre, building up the sides (if you're not using a cake tin, pipe or spoon the mixture on to the circle on the plate in the same way). Bake for about 1 hour at 300°F (150°C or gas 2), then remove very carefully and allow to cool. Fill with any kind of fruit.

**Home sweet home**

These last two recipes are for rare moments of motherhood when everything is sweetness, light, and love; the kids are fine and have just had good school reports; your bad back is better and you've just had your hair done. In short, everything is lovely. So is home-made ice-cream:

375 ml (¾ pint) custard (made with 1½ tablespoons custard powder, or use the Never-fail custard recipe on page 54)
50 g (2 oz) sugar
125 ml (5 fl oz or ¼ pint) whipped cream, or whipped chilled evaporated milk
1 teaspoon vanilla essence
2 egg whites left over from real custard (optional)

Set the refrigerator to the coldest point at least half an hour before you start. Mix all the ingredients together. (If egg whites are left over from your custard, whisk these stiff and fold into the mixture.) Pour into freezing trays and freeze till firm, then take out, whisk furiously again, and re-freeze. Mothers who have a deep freeze can really make the most of this by doubling or quadrupling the recipe.

**Chocolate ice-cream**

1 large tin evaporated milk
3 level tablespoons caster sugar
1 level teaspoon powdered gelatine dissolved in 1 tablespoon water
75 g (3 oz) plain chocolate dissolved in 3 tablespoons of water
½ teaspoon vanilla essence

Set the refrigerator to its coldest point first. Mix the evaporated milk with the sugar, stir in the dissolved gelatine and pour into freezing trays. Freeze for about 1½ hours, or until crystals begin to form, then take out, pour into a chilled mixing bowl and whisk until thick. Now fold in the chocolate mixture and the vanilla, pour it back into the freezing trays and freeze it hard. If your refrigerator refuses to co-operate, forget the whole thing and use the mixture as sauce for the ice-cream you buy from the nice man who drives the van with musical chimes.

And after all that, it's a fact that kids can even go off ice-cream. From babyhood children like puddings because they're sweet. But, as they get older, they become faddier and faddier, sometimes to the point where they don't actually like puddings much at all. If you catch them at that crucial point you may be able to let puddings slide into oblivion altogether. Keep trying.

# 5 Teas

Whatever children call their last meal of the day – tea, supper, dinner – it can seem like the last straw to mothers. If it has been a big day (when you're a mother, every day is a big day), everyone is tired. Pretty soon dad will be home, probably tired too, and as hungry as anybody. Official fixtures like 'teatime' and 'suppertime' blur into the kind of late-day scramble known to mothers and rush-hour motorists.

It takes a bran-tub mentality to plan and get through this meal, so this chapter is a bran-tub from which to pick ideas. First, 'low' teas for very young children; simple meals of the cheese-on-toast and scrambled-egg variety. Then 'high' teas for older kids, with soups, a selection of pastas, and savoury supper dishes. And finally a batch of home bakes at the end.

Just a word, before we fall into the bran-tub, about those home bakes. Many a mum gets a genuine creative kick out of baking, and no woman worth her salt would scorn a domestic activity which has both a delicious end product and some sense of the practical about it. But at tea, just as at every other meal, mums do well to go easy on the carbohydrates. If the first and last meals of the day consist only of starchy foods – cereal and toast at breakfast; jam scones and cake for tea – then a child is getting protein only once a day: at midday.

It's not enough. Protein foods like meat, fish, chicken, eggs, and cheese should be eaten in some form three times a day; tea is no exception to the rule of balance. Protein teas for little children are easier to think up because the 1½-5-year-old age-group like trusty favourites that are more or less a variation on the balanced breakfast theme. Besides that – if mums are conscientious about it – children at home eat a proper midday meal every day. But older children, five and upwards, cause us to scrabble despairingly for variety as the afternoon draws on to the high spot of tea.

Older children burn more energy; they grow fast in fits and starts; they need more food and, because they may shovel down carbohydrates by the truckload, they need big doses of protein to even things out. The food they eat at school can be hard to account for. It is not uncommon for a nine-year-old to dazzle his mother for weeks with the impressive catalogue of meat, green vegetables, and fruit he gets at school, omitting to mention that all he actually eats are the potatoes and the sponge pud.

So tea is an important meal. It's important from the sociability point of view, too. Tea is when mothers hear the latest crop of terrible jokes from the school playground, the moaning about Form Two's maths test and the news that my friend Fanny who had a runny nose yesterday has measles today, mum.

Cooking and serving two suppers every evening is no joke, and that's another good reason for making 'low' teas for little ones both early and simple. No sooner has the last banana skin fallen on the floor than mum has to start cooking for dad with one hand, while wrestling the kids into bath and bed with the other. It's all work, and a lot of it, and it's no wonder we wind up cross and frazzled at the very moment our husbands expect us to be like those serene mothers in the magazines. It seems sensible, as soon as the children are old enough, to plan a combined meal for both children and adults, even if parents' conversation is shot through with kids' squabbles.

All the 'high' tea recipes given here do double duty for family meals and a lot are interchangeable with the main courses in Chapter 2. If, having nosed through the earlier chapters, you have been wondering what happened to sausages, spaghetti, and other life-savers, you need look no further. They're all here.

## LOW TEAS

Here is a run-down of ideas for teas for children up to the age of about five.

### French toast

3 standard-size eggs
3 tablespoons milk
4 thick slices trimmed bread

Break the eggs into a shallow bowl and whisk in the milk. Dunk the bread slices in this mixture and when they are soggy fry on both sides, in a little butter or oil, until golden brown. Serve with maple syrup, or golden syrup, or honey or jam. French toast is good at breakfast, too.

### Angel cushions

Seasoned mashed potato (left-over is fine)
2 or 3 eggs
100-150 g (4-6 oz) grated cheese

Beat these ingredients into a gooey mess and drop dessertspoons of the mixture into hot oil. Fry until golden brown and get set to answer a lot of searching questions about why angels need cushions. ('Because they get tired – like me' is a fast answer.)

### Egg lick

This is for the small child who won't touch eggs boiled, scrambled, baked, coddled, or prayed over. Mix an egg or two in a huge mixing bowl with a teaspoon of sugar and half a teaspoon of flour. Smear it over the sides, pretend you have just made a cake and let the child persuade you to allow him to lick out the bowl.

### Scrabble

4 large eggs
100 g (4 oz or about a cupful) cooked chopped green beans, or carrots, or bacon bits, or anything interesting and tasty
a little salt and pepper
fat for frying (bacon fat is nice)

Break the eggs and mix them lightly together with the seasoning. Melt the fat in a frying pan, add the chopped bits and stir in the egg mixture. Keep stirring with a wooden spoon until the eggs begin to scramble, then serve quickly before they overcook. Scrabble should be on the runny side.

### Oven-baked omelette

By the end of a rough day many a mum is ready to put her own head in the oven rather than anything else. Don't. Put this omelette in instead and by the time the kids are bathed it will be ready and you'll feel a lot better.

25 g (1 oz) butter
5 or 6 standard eggs
50 g (2 oz) grated cheese (or chopped ham, or chopped cooked vegetables)
2 tomatoes, skinned (see page 42) and sliced
1 teaspoon chopped parsley
salt and pepper

Heat the butter for a few minutes in a large, shallow ovenproof dish. Beat the eggs lightly together and season well. Stir in the grated cheese (or chopped bits), add the tomatoes and parsley and pour the lot into the buttery dish. Bake uncovered at 425-450°F (220-230°C or gas 7-8) for 10-15 minutes. By this time the mixture should be set. Ovens vary, so keep an eye on this the first time you make it, and note how long it actually takes.

**Cheesy spread**

Cheese spreads are expensive to buy and it's a bore to have to grate cheese for rarebits. You can make your own spread, which will keep for a month in a covered jar in the refrigerator, and use it for all kinds of cheese flavouring – on toast, spread over pastas, in sandwiches, or thinned down with milk to make a sauce. Double or treble this mixture as you need.

2 beaten eggs
500 g (1 lb) grated Cheddar cheese
1 teaspoon powdered mustard
a little more than 250 ml (½ pint) milk
25 g (1 oz) butter or marge
salt and pepper

Beat the eggs lightly in a saucepan and stir in the cheese, mustard, and milk. Add the butter or marge, season, and stir steadily over moderate heat. When the mixture begins to thicken, pour it into a jar and let it cool. As it cools it will get much thicker. Finally cover and refrigerate.

**Sausage surprise**

500 g (1 lb) sausage meat
4 eggs
4 rashers bacon (or a couple of sliced tomatoes)

Grease an ovenproof dish and spread the sausage meat thickly on the bottom. Press four hollows in the meat with the back of the spoon and break an egg into each one. Lay the bacon rashers or tomato slices over the top and bake for 20-25 minutes at 400°F (200°C, gas 6) until the eggs are cooked. This is good served with potato crisps, followed by fruit.

### Pretend pizza

4 thick slices of bread, trimmed and cut into rounds
3 or 4 tomatoes
a few sliced gherkins (optional, and very risky)
100 g (4 oz) grated cheese (or the cheese mix on page 75)
4 bacon rashers, cut in strips (or strips of ham, luncheon meat, or similar)

Toast the bread slices on one side only and butter the untoasted side. On the buttered side, arrange the sliced tomato (and gherkins, if you dare), sprinkle or spread with cheese and lay the strips of meat over the top in a lattice pattern. Grill under medium heat for 5 minutes or so and serve hot.

### Kids' kebabs

Most children will eat almost anything if it comes on a stick. You'll need a hot grill, a selection of bite-sized pieces of food, and a skewer or steel knitting needle per child. *No other metal will do* (let alone plastic needles, which one of us was once crazy enough to try). Combinations of food are almost limitless and amounts depend on the day's demand. You might try one or two of these to get your hand in:

pieces of sausage threaded with baby tomatoes
cubes of beef, or lamb, or liver, or kidney, or luncheon meat threaded with pieces of veg – celery, onion, mushroom, carrot
bits of cooked ham threaded with pineapple chunks or cooked prunes
banana chunks wrapped in bacon rashers

If one kind of food takes longer to cook, start grilling it first and add the other bits later. Remember to brush everything with oil first, and turn the kebabs occasionally so that they cook all over.

## HIGH TEAS

Everything in this section is suitable for kids over the age of five or so; all of them are fine for family meals at any time. First come soups and easy starters, then pastas, then a few slightly more complicated knife-and-fork affairs for high tea.

As a kick-off, here is an idea for those of us who are suckers for family co-operation, togetherness, all the progressive doctrines about child-raising which bring tears to maternal eyes because they sound so lovely and in practice so seldom work. It's a triumph of hope over experience that some of us keep on trying.

### Self-service supper

Get the children to prepare, or help to prepare, a tray covered with a selection of:

sliced cold meats
sliced salami, liver sausage, or similar
sliced cheeses
salad ingredients
raw vegetables (carrots, celery, radishes)
a variety of breads and/or savoury biscuits

Any child over seven should be able to use a knife safely – to be sure, give him a blunt one and let him chop cheese chunks for practice. Allocating particular foods to each child will help to reduce fighting; and if the finished tray is a muddle and a mess it doesn't matter; they'll enjoy doing it and will eat much more if allowed to help themselves. Finish up with a bowl of nuts and dried fruit.

### Leek-and-celery soup

2 large leeks
1 small head of celery
2 peeled potatoes
25 g (1 oz) butter or marge
1 litre (1000 ml or 2 pints) chicken stock (use stock cubes)
salt and pepper
chopped parsley

Wash the leeks well and chop them, including the green part. Wash and chop the celery and slice the potatoes thinly. Melt the fat in a large saucepan and fry the leeks and celery until lightly browned. Now pitch in the potato slices, some seasoning, and pour in the stock. Simmer gently for 45 minutes, then serve with the parsley sprinkled on top. This is a good chunky soup. It liquidizes into a good creamy one.

### All-gone-away soup

You can put this into a dead-low oven at 9 a.m., go out for the day, and by 5 p.m. when the kids are tired and cold and in no mood to hang around waiting for tea, tea will be hanging around waiting for them. Put all these ingredients into a big saucepan:

- 250-500 g (8-16 oz) washed and drained lentils (or dried split peas). If you like your soup even thicker, add more
- 2 large onions, finely chopped
- 2 large carrots, grated or chopped fine
- 1½ litres (3 pints) of stock
- some chopped bacon rashers
- salt and pepper

Bring all this to the boil. Now pour it into a large casserole, cover, and leave in the oven at its lowest setting. It'll take about 8 hours to cook, but an extra hour or more won't hurt.

### Creamy corn soup

- 1 tin (226 g or 8 oz) creamed sweet corn
- 1 finely chopped onion
- 250 ml (½ pint) water or stock
- 1 tablespoon (25 g or 1 oz) cornflour
- 250 ml (½ pint) milk
- salt and pepper
- chopped parsley or grated cheese

Put the creamed corn and the onion into a saucepan, add the water or stock, and cook gently until the onion is tender. Mix the cornflour with a little of the milk, then add the rest and pour the mixture into the soup. Bring to the boil, stirring hard, then simmer for 5 minutes. Season and serve sprinkled with parsley or grated cheese. You can jazz this up with tuna or any cooked flaked fish, or chunks of cooked ham or bacon, for a fully-fledged meal.

### Chow chowder

- a piece of marge, for frying
- 1 large chopped onion
- 3 potatoes, peeled and diced
- 125 ml (5 fl oz or ¼ pint) boiling water
- 375 ml (¾ pint) milk
- salt and pepper
- grated cheese
- chopped parsley
- 250 g (8 oz) shelled prawns (more if you can afford it; or cooked cubed fish)

That looks like an awful lot of ingredients, but this is a quick, filling, and delicious soup. Melt the marge and fry the chopped onion in it until tender but not brown. Put in the diced potato, the water and seasoning, cover the pan and simmer gently for 15 minutes. Add the prawns (or cooked fish) and the milk, and bring the soup back to the boil. Simmer gently for another 10 minutes and then stir in the grated cheese and parsley.

**Budget broth**

3 large onions, peeled and sliced
a little cooking oil
3 peeled tomatoes (page 42)
1 litre (2 pints) stock (or water with one stock cube)
salt and pepper
1 teaspoon sugar
grated cheese

Fry the sliced onions in oil until tender, with the lid on the pan. Slice the tomatoes and throw them in, then add the stock, seasoning, and sugar. Simmer gently for half-an-hour. Serve hot with grated cheese to sprinkle over the top.

These next two are quick and easy if you have a blender and quite a hassle if you don't. But they still work with the ingredients chopped as fine as possible. Older children like rough, terrine-like patés as much as smooth ones – but skip them both if they look too much like work. Otherwise serve with hot buttered toast.

**Natty paté**

250 g (½ lb) diced liver sausage
2 tablespoons mayonnaise or salad cream
2 tablespoons top-of-the-milk (or cream, if you have it)
a squeeze of lemon
salt and pepper

Put all this into a blender and whizz for half a minute. (Or chop the liver sausage as finely as possible and mix everything like mad.)

**Chicken liver paté**

This will keep for several days in a covered jar in the refrigerator while you try to remember to buy some more crackers to smear it on.

300 g (10 oz) chicken livers
75 g (3 oz) butter
1 small chopped onion
a pinch of dried herbs
a little salt (garlic salt, if possible) and pepper

Brown the chicken livers lightly in about half the butter; then take them out of the pan and fry the chopped onion for a few minutes. Put back the livers, add the herbs and seasoning, and cook the whole lot very gently, under a lid, for 5 minutes. Now scrape it all into the blender with the rest of the butter and blend until smooth. This can be eaten right away, but is better piled in a bowl and left to chill for a while.

The next two recipes can start and finish a meal equally well; both are perfectly delicious. The first one sounds and tastes Swiss.

## Yodel

1 medium-sized carton (125 ml or 5 fl oz) natural yoghurt
2 heaped tablespoons porridge oats
1 apple, not peeled, but cored and chopped
1 orange, peeled, pipped, and chopped
2 tablespoons (75 g or 3 oz) sultanas
brown sugar to taste

Mix all these ingredients together and throw in a few chopped nuts. Chill in the refrigerator for a couple of hours if you can.

## Grilled grapefruit

4 grapefruit halves
4 tablespoons brown sugar

Take out the pips and cut round the edges of the grapefruit to loosen the segments. Cover each half with brown sugar and grill under medium heat for 10-15 minutes.

If *Pastas* didn't exist, mothers would be in serious trouble. As it is, we're in business and calling down blessings on the Italian mamas who undoubtedly invented the stuff. Spaghetti, noodles, macaroni, and lasagne (by no means all the pastas, but a representative selection) cook in lots of boiling water to which a swish of salt and a drip of cooking oil should be added. The oil prevents the stuff sticking into a gluey clump, but you should also give pasta a good stir round when you have dropped it in. *Don't cook for too long;* 15 minutes is usually long enough; and in any case you should fish out a piece and bite it to see that it is still chewy in the middle – it ought to be.

Cooked pasta should be eaten right away, but it's possible to tide it over a short delay by tossing it in a nugget of butter after draining.

There are as many ways of making spaghetti sauce in Italy as there are changes of government. We have just one; it comes either with meat or without. Here it is without.

### Spaghetti sauce without

25 g (1 oz) butter
1 medium-sized onion, finely chopped
1 small tin (141 g or 5 oz) tomato purée
salt and pepper
1 tablespoon water
grated cheese for serving

Melt the butter and gently cook the chopped onion until it is soft but not brown. Add the purée, salt and pepper, and the water and stir round to make a buttery, tomato-y, oniony glaze. Meanwhile, 250 g (8 oz) of spaghetti is simmering peacefully in another saucepan for the required 12-15 minutes. When this is ready, drain it and add it to the sauce. Now grab a couple of forks and toss the spaghetti until the strands are covered with the hot tomato and butter. Turn it all into a heated dish and scatter on the grated cheese. This is a meal on its own; or you can make it really substantial and serve it with grilled sausages, or cold ham, or fried eggs. Kids love it at any age.

### Spaghetti sauce with

10 g (½ oz) butter, marge, or oil
1 chopped onion
2-3 rashers chopped bacon (optional)

100 g (¼ lb) mince
1 can (226 g or 8 oz) peeled tomatoes (or purée)
1 tablespoon stock or wine (or 125 ml (5 fl oz or ¼ pint) stock, if you're using the purée)
1 teaspoon sugar
salt (garlic salt for choice) and pepper
grated cheese for serving

Fry the chopped onion and bacon lightly in the fat or oil, then put in the meat and fry that, breaking it up with a fork as you go. Pour in the can of tomatoes (or tomato purée), and add the right amount of liquid along with the sugar, salt, and pepper. Simmer the sauce for 20-30 minutes while you cook whatever pasta you have on the shelf today. Dish up the pasta when it's done, then either pour the sauce over the top or serve it in a separate bowl. The grated cheese is for the kids to sprinkle over their platefuls.

**Lah-sah-nyah** (for 6)

Lasagne comes in flat, wide strips; either spaghetti-coloured or pale green (the spinach lasagne), and it breaks if you look at it (which doesn't matter a bit but tends to sap the confidence and make many a mum want to fling the stuff at the wall). It makes a marvellous meat-sauce-and-pasta casserole, well worth cooking in large quantities for a mob of hungry children; or, if you have a freezer, to freeze in batches against those days when you can scarcely summon up the strength to prise open a freezer door, let alone get tea. You'll need a certain amount of strength to make it, since it takes a clear half-hour; and you'll also need two sauces and the agility of an eel – which is how cooked lasagne feels and behaves – to pull it all together. It's worth it.

250 g (8 oz) lasagne
a double quantity of Spaghetti Sauce With on page 81
500 ml (1 pint) white sauce, flavoured with 100 g (4 oz) grated cheese
about 100 g (4 oz) extra grated cheese

Put the lasagne strips into plenty of boiling salted water, to which you have added a drip of oil, in your biggest saucepan. Simmer for 15 minutes, then drain and tip it into a bowl of cold water, which will both prevent the strips sticking together and cool them down sufficiently for you to pick them up – and you're going to *have* to pick them up. By this time you have made your Spaghetti Sauce With and your cheese-flavoured white sauce and are beginning to get bored with all this cooking, but having come so far, you're stuck with it. Turn the oven to 375°F (190°C or gas 5) and soldier on.

Line a shallow greased baking dish or casserole with some cooked lasagne strips. Now smear a layer of Spaghetti Sauce With over the top, followed by a layer of cheesy white sauce. Now a second layer of lasagne, a second layer of 'With' and a second layer of white sauce. And so on until you run dry, finishing with a layer of lasagne. Top this with a layer of grated cheese and bake for 40 minutes. And that's it. Serve either hot or cold, and watch it go.

As a postscript to this one, you can use chopped cooked chicken instead of the Spaghetti Sauce With; and a couple of cans of condensed mushroom soup, undiluted, instead of the white sauce. Granted it's a lot quicker; but we never have that much left-over chicken. We only have a little bit, and that goes into:

### Risotto

Which is basically rice cooked in stock, with as many little bits of meat, chicken, fish, shellfish, liver, kidneys, bacon, mushroom, and chopped cooked veg as you can juggle together. Start here.

1 chopped onion
a knob of butter or marge
250-350 g (8-10 oz) rice – long grain patna-type
any and all chopped left-overs except potato
a few extras in the way of chopped bacon, ham, liver, prawns or whatever
a tin (226 g or 8 oz) peeled tomatoes
500-750 ml (1-1½ pints) chicken stock – made from stock cubes
about 50 g (2 oz) grated cheese

Fry the chopped onion gently in the butter in a large saucepan or casserole. Add the rice and stir it round for a few minutes until it is buttery but not brown. Now pitch in all the bits and pieces of protein you can lay your hands on, pour in the tomatoes, and fill up with the stock. Stir well, then simmer very gently for about 30 minutes until the rice is soft. Stir in the cheese at the end, brushing aside any child's churlish remark about a dish whose appearance is a good deal less than pretty. Risotto is very tasty stuff and scraped plates will prove it.

### Pop pilaff

Which is boiled rice with a hole in the middle. Plug the hole with this sauce.

- 250 g (½ lb) cubed liver (or 250 g (½ lb) kidney skinned, cored, and cubed)
- 4 rashers bacon, chopped into pieces
- 1 chopped onion
- 250 ml (½ pint) chicken stock
- 1 tablespoon (10 g or ½ oz) cornflour
- salt and pepper
- 250 g (8 oz) cooked rice for serving

Cut everything up fairly small, then fry the liver or kidney, bacon, and onion all together in a little oil until the onion is soft. Pour on the stock and simmer gently for about 20 minutes. Meanwhile start cooking the rice in plenty of boiling salted water. It will take 10-12 minutes, and when it is done you can drain it and leave it under a clean dry cloth to dry out a little. Finally mix the cornflour with a little water and stir it into the pilaff mixture. Check the seasoning, then arrange the rice in a border around a dish and pile the pilaff mixture in the middle.

Now here are a couple of hefty teas using sausage meat.

### Rock'n'roll

- 1 packet (212 g or 7½ oz) frozen puff or short pastry
- 500 g (1 lb) sausage meat (or 250 g (½ lb) sausage meat and 250 g (½ lb) chopped bacon rashers)
- 2 chopped onions
- salt and pepper
- a little milk

Roll out the pastry into a rectangle about 30 cm by 23 cm (12 in. × 9 in.). Mix the meat with the chopped onions and seasoning and form this into a big sausage about 25·5 cm (10 in.) long. Place this on the pastry, then wet the edges, roll up and seal. Make three small slits on the top with a knife, brush over with milk, and bake at 375°F (190°C or gas 5) for an hour. Kids like ketchup or apple sauce with this.

**Roly-poly eggs**

4 hard-boiled eggs
375 g (¾ lb) sausage meat
3-4 tablespoons (75 g or 3 oz) seasoned flour
1 beaten egg
4 tablespoons (75 g or 3 oz) breadcrumbs

Shell the eggs and cover them *all over* with the sausage meat – don't leave any chinks. Roll them in the flour, then in the beaten egg, then in the breadcrumbs. Now roll in all three again in the same order. Deep-fry in deep, very hot fat or oil until golden brown, and keep the children well out of the way while you're doing it. Allow to cool down a little on greaseproof paper, then serve cut in half with a salad; or keep them whole for later. They're good for picnics, too.

**Sneaky soufflé**

This is a soufflé topping that you can bake on top of almost anything – chicken, tuna, baked beans, most vegetables – and feel happy about because the kids are getting egg and cheese and milk too. It's not a proper soufflé, and being baked on a lumpy base may not improve its appearance, but who cares. We don't; and neither will the children.

25 g (1 oz) butter
25 g (1 oz) flour
125 ml (5 fl oz or ¼ pint) milk
2 eggs
50 g (2 oz) grated cheese (or cheesy spread, page 75)
a little salt and pepper

Melt the butter gently in a saucepan over low heat, then take the pan off the heat and stir in the flour. Mix in the milk, then return to low heat for a minute or so, stirring madly as the sauce thickens and comes to the boil. Now park on one side while you separate the eggs. Beat some of the sauce into the yolks, then add them to the rest of the sauce along with the grated cheese or cheese spread, and beat everything together with seasoning. Whisk the egg whites stiff and fold into the sauce, and finally pour the lot over whatever you have spread over the bottom of a buttered casserole dish. Bake at 400°F (200°C or gas 6) for 25 minutes, and serve right away.

**Pancakes**

You'll find both recipe and cooking method in Chapter 4 on page 59. Here is the basic recipe again, along with some suggested fillings for tea. We have to say here and now that pancakes *are* worth the tired feet that are the by-product of making a batch. Make them any time and make as many as you can – they'll keep for 3 or 4 days in the refrigerator between layers of greaseproof paper parcelled in foil; and they freeze beautifully. The quantities given are for 8 pancakes. Double or treble as you need.

100 g (4 oz) plain flour
a pinch of salt
1 egg
250-260 ml (½ pint) milk – or half-milk half-water
a knob of melted butter

Turn back to page 59 for mixing and cooking methods.

**Pancake fillings**

These combinations, and any other variations you come up with, can be added to 250 ml (½ pint) of well-seasoned white sauce made with half-milk half-stock. If you can start the sauce by frying some chopped onion in the butter or marge first, so much the better. When you have filled and rolled up the pancakes, lay them in a shallow dish, cover with a lid or foil, and heat them through in a slow to moderate oven for half-an-hour. Make sure the cover fits; pancakes can go leathery if uncovered for longer than a few minutes. Just before serving you can whip off the cover, sprinkle on some grated cheese and brown quickly under the grill.

*Corned beef and celery:* about 375 g (12 oz) diced corned beef mixed with some sticks of thinly sliced celery and a teaspoon of French mustard

*Spinach and bacon:* a packet of frozen spinach cooked and mixed with 250 g (½ lb) chopped fried bacon

*Fish and egg:* about 250 g (½ lb) cooked and flaked smoked haddock mixed with 2 chopped hard-boiled eggs and chopped parsley

*Tuna (or chicken) and sweetcorn:* a can of flaked tuna (or some chopped cooked chicken) mixed with a can of sweetcorn

*Sausage and mushroom:* 250 g (½ lb) cooked sausages, thinly sliced, mixed with 100 g (¼ lb) sliced uncooked mushrooms

*Pork (or ham, or bacon) and beans:* about 250 g (½ lb) diced cooked pork (or ham or bacon) mixed with a packet of cooked and diced frozen French beans

*Cheese pancakes:* stack the pancakes one on top of the other, spreading cheese sauce between each layer; finish with a dollop of sauce

Pushing pancakes even further (but not forgetting the tired feet), check back to Puddings, page 60, for a variety of sweet fillings. Jam with a dab of whipped cream; ice-cream with flaked chocolate; apple sauce with cinnamon; a squeeze of plain old lemon juice with a sprinkle of plain old sugar. There is no need to add sugar to the basic batter recipe for any of these.

Few things madden mothers more than a recipe which calmly calls for a pastry flan case – unless it is the recipe which has the nerve to *assume that you actually have one ready baked* (see page 58). Flan cases take time; they are messy to make; the children invariably get wind that pastry is in the making and hurtle to your elbow to demand that you give them the hard-won dough to make yet another batch of grubby Scotty-dogs (with charred raisins for eyes) which mothers have been choking down for generations. You can short-circuit the whole business of flan cases for savoury fillings by using this invaluable notion again and again.

**Cracker flan**

100 g (4 oz) melted butter
125 g (5 oz) crumbled cream crackers

Mix the cracker crumbs into the melted butter and press the mixture into a pie dish. That's all. It works. Fill with any of the lovely suggestions offered in the infuriating recipes which call for a flan case. Here's a lovely one to start on.

### Cock-a-snook flan filling

1 finely chopped onion
4 (or more) rashers chopped bacon
2 eggs
pepper
250 ml (½ pint) milk
250 g (8 oz) grated cheese

Fry the chopped onion and bacon together until the onion is lightly brown, and spread the mixture over the flan base. Now beat up the eggs with a little pepper, mix in the milk and grated cheese, and pour this over the onion and bacon. Bake at 325°F (170°C or gas 3) for 45 minutes, until set and browned on top. This is good hot or cold.

### Conscience-smitten supper stew (for 6-8)

Here's a stew which rams home the point about not being able to count on children eating well or sensibly at school. If, at around noon, you imagine them pushing aside the protein and vitamins and facing a long afternoon on two bites of potato, it might spur you on to put this into a low oven for 3½ hours or so. It's not cheap, but it pays off a score of anxious doubts.

1 kg (1000 g or 2 lb) good stewing beef
3 or 4 carrots
2 large onions
1 medium tin (298 g or 10½ oz) condensed oxtail soup
250 ml (½ pint) water
a few mixed herbs
bay leaf
salt and pepper

Cut the beef into cubes, then prepare and chop the vegetables. Dilute the soup with the water, and then put everything into a large casserole, stir it around well, and cook covered for 3½ hours at 275°F (140°C or gas 1). Serve with a healthy tomato salad. If the kids aren't as keen as you are on this gesture of loving concern, heat it through slowly next day and serve for supper with questions about who ate what at school.

And finally, here are some favourite ways of packaging carbohydrates for children whose protein intake is well up to par.

### Scones

250 g (8 oz) self-raising flour
1 level teaspoon baking powder
a good pinch of salt
50 g (2 oz) butter or marge
1½ tablespoons (20 g or ½-1 oz) caster sugar
1 egg
4 tablespoons (75 ml or 3 fl oz) milk

Sift the flour, baking powder, and salt. Now rub in the butter and mix in the sugar. Beat the egg into the milk and add slowly to the mixture, mixing to a soft dough. Turn on to a lightly-floured board, knead the dough briefly, then roll out to about 1 cm (½ in.) thick and cut into rounds with a pastry cutter or glass. Lay on a *hot* baking tray, brush with milk and bake for 12-15 minutes at 450°F (230°C or gas 8). Split and spread with butter when they have cooled. If you want these to eat later, they store well in an airtight tin for a day or two; or freeze in plastic bags. You can vary the recipe by substituting 100 g (4 oz) grated cheese for the sugar.

### Instant cheese muffins

From first thought to last bite, these take about 15 minutes to cook and eat. Don't store them. They should be eaten right away.

100 g (4 oz) plain flour
100 g (4 oz) grated cheese
2 level teaspoons baking powder
1 teaspoon salt
a little milk

Mix the dry ingredients together, adding just a little milk to reach a dough-like consistency. Now roll out about 2 cm (¾ in.) thick, and cut into rounds. Bake at 450°F (230°C or gas 8) for 7-10 minutes, then split, butter, and serve hot.

## Drop scones

100 g (4 oz) flour
1 tablespoon sugar
1 teaspoon baking soda
1½ teaspoons cream of tartar
1 egg
100 ml (4 fl oz) milk

Sift the dry ingredients together, then make a well in the centre, break in the egg and start mixing, adding the milk in slurps as you go. The batter should be of the consistency of cream. Drop spoonfuls of batter on to a lightly-greased hot pan or skillet. When the tops start to bubble, flip over and cook the other side for about a minute. Serve hot, with cream and jam.

## Taffy's teacakes

A reliable and relaxing recipe, for a soft rock bun.

250 g (8 oz) flour
1 teaspoon cream-of-tartar
½ teaspoon baking soda
a pinch of salt
3 tablespoons (75 g or 3 oz) sugar
75 g (3 oz) butter or marge
100 g (4 oz) cleaned, mixed dried fruit
1 egg
5 tablespoons (75-100 ml) milk

Sift flour, cream-of-tartar, baking soda and salt into a bowl and stir in the sugar. Rub in the butter, then mix in the dried fruit. Now make a well in the centre, break in the egg and start stirring with a wooden spoon, adding the milk and mixing to a soft dough.

At this point you can roll it out and cut into rounds. Don't bother. Put dessertspoons of the dough into the greased hollows of a bun tin (or baking cases placed on a baking sheet) and bake at 350°F (180°C or gas 3-4) for 20-30 minutes. Split, butter, and serve. These keep well in an airtight tin if you want to store them for a while.

## Flapjacks

Easy, delicious, and popular enough to disappear by the plateful unless you double the recipe and hide the extra batch in an airtight tin for another day.

150 g (6 oz) butter or marge
150 g (6 oz) demerara sugar
150 g (6 oz) oatmeal (porridge oats)

Melt the butter and sugar together over low heat and mix in the oats. Spread the mixture on a shallow, greased baking tin about 20 cm × 30 cm (8 in. × 12 in.) and bake at 375°F (190°C or gas 5) for about 20 minutes. Take out and mark in squares while hot, then allow to cool. When completely cold, carefully lift the squares out of the tin.

### Chocolate cheat cookies

Rattling around the bottom of every family biscuit tin is a disreputable collection of broken bits, crumbs, and unloved rejects. If you can lay your hands on a spare tin, and remember to pitch all biscuit left-overs into it over a period, you'll accumulate enough to make this recipe. (We reckon on twice a year or so, being not over-scrupulous about including half-chewed biscuits left on plates.)

300 g (10 oz) broken biscuit bits
125 g (5 oz) margarine
25 g (1 oz) sugar
75 g (3 oz) drinking chocolate powder, or 35 g (1½ oz) cocoa
2-3 tablespoons (75-100 g) golden syrup

*Icing*
250 g (8 oz) cooking chocolate

Crush the biscuit bits into crumbs, either by pounding them in a mixing bowl with a blunt object, or rolling them with a rolling pin. Melt the marge, sugar, drinking chocolate powder, and syrup all together in a pan over low heat, then stir in the biscuit crumbs. Grease a shallow baking tin about 20 cm × 30 cm (8 in. × 12 in.), and press the biscuit mixture into it, then leave to cool. When it has set, melt the cooking chocolate in a bowl over hot water and smooth this over the top. When cold, cut into fingers and ease the cookies out of the tin with a knife.

### Bran loaf

Some enchanted evening when the kids are washing the dishes for you, you might mix together the following ingredients and leave them to soak overnight:

50 g (2 oz) All-Bran cereal
100 g (4 oz) soft brown sugar
125 g (5 oz) mixed dried fruit
150 ml (6 fl oz) milk

In the morning stir 75 g (3 oz) self-raising flour into the mixture and bake in a greased loaf tin at 300°F (150°C or gas 2) for an hour. Cool thoroughly before slicing.

### Mrs McClure's Irish barmbrack

Another old soak to leave overnight and deal with in the morning.

125-250 ml (¼-½ pint) warm tea
500 g (1 lb) mixed dried fruit
250 g (8 oz) sugar, preferably brown
500 g (1 lb) self-raising flour
1 teaspoon mixed spice
50 g (2 oz) marge
1 egg
2 tablespoons marmalade

Soak the dried fruit and sugar overnight in the tea. In the morning sift the flour with the spice and rub in the marge. Stir in the egg, then add the fruit mixture and the marmalade and mix well. Bake in a large well-greased tin or 2 loaf tins at 325°F (170°C or gas 3) for 1½-2 hours while you hustle through the housework and have another cup of tea to fortify nerves jangling with the shock of baking in the morning. Let the barmbrack cool thoroughly before cutting.

### Gingerbread

250 g (8 oz) flour
1 teaspoon mixed spice
1 teaspoon baking soda
2 teaspoons ground ginger
250 g (8 oz) demerara sugar
100 g (4 oz) marge
4 tablespoons black treacle
1 small egg, beaten into 250 ml (½ pint) milk

Sift the dry ingredients together while you melt the marge, treacle, and sugar together in a fairly large saucepan over low heat. Now stir alternate dollops of dry mix and egg-and-milk into the sticky syrup, and pour into a greased lined loaf tin. Bake at 350°F (180°C or gas 4) for about an hour. Allow to cool, then ease a knife around the sides and turn out.

### Best buttercake

250 g (8 oz) unsalted butter
250 g (8 oz) caster sugar
4 eggs
250 g (8 oz) self-raising flour
125 g (5 oz) cleaned, mixed dried fruit
1 tablespoon sherry (optional)

Cream the butter and sugar together, then beat in the eggs one at a time. Sift the flour and fold it into the mixture by tablespoonfuls, and gradually fold in the dried fruit. If you're using the sherry stir it in now (or swig it instead, as a bracer against the cost of these extravagant ingredients), and then stir the whole thing well. Grease a 20 cm (8 in.) cake tin and line it with greaseproof paper, then pour in the mixture and bake at 325°F (170°C or gas 3) for about 1¼-1½ hours. It's a good cake.

**Chocolate fudge cake**

If the kids can wait for this to cool down they'll get a delicious chewy cake; if they can't wait, it makes a good hot pudding to serve with custard sauce or ice-cream.

100 g (4 oz) marge
250 g (10 oz) sugar
2 eggs
150 g (6 oz) flour
50 g (2 oz) cocoa powder
a drop or two of vanilla essence

Melt the marge in a big saucepan, then add the sugar and the beaten eggs. Stir in the flour, cocoa, and vanilla essence. Now grease and line a shallow tin with greaseproof paper (about 18 cm (7 in.) square is ideal) and pour in the mixture. Bake at 350°F (180°C or gas 4) for 30-40 minutes. Cut into squares when cold, and lift out of the tin.

**Moody mum's soda bread**

The urge to bake bread at home rises in most of us – usually around the time when domestic gadgetry goes haywire, the economic outlook is black, and the whole business of modern living seems too complicated to cope with. It's an urge which, unchecked, can blossom into weaving our own tweed, throwing our own pots, even retreating to a remote country homestead to grow our own turnips and singe our own eyebrows trying to light our own lamps. Baking bread is fine – in moderation. Especially when it doesn't involve *yeast* – the mysteries of which make modern living look like simplicity itself. Here's a no-yeast recipe which works with no trouble and makes us feel – if only temporarily – that we have atoned for all those tins and packets of convenience food served up to the children.

250 g (½ lb) plain white flour
100 g (¼ lb) plain brown flour
½ teaspoon salt
½ teaspoon bicarbonate of soda
½ teaspoon caster sugar
25 g (1 oz) marge
1 egg
125 ml (5 fl oz or ¼ pint) thick sour milk (fresh milk can be soured with a squeeze of lemon juice)

Sift the dry ingredients together and rub the marge into the mixture. Beat the egg with the sour milk and mix it in lightly. Now knead the mixture well – it should be soft but not dry. Shape into a flat round on a floured baking sheet and cut a cross over the top. Bake in the middle of a hot oven, 425°F (220°C or gas 7) for half an hour. Take out, wrap in a clean, damp tea towel and stand on a rack to cool. (This mixture makes good rolls too. Bake 10-15 minutes at the same temperature.)

While it's cooling, and your satisfaction fairly glowing, spare a thought for mothers who not only *have* to bake their own bread, but also have to collect the sticks to light the fire to heat the oven to bake it in. Modern living has its good points.

# 6 Parties

Of the many trials and joys of motherhood, giving a children's party is up there in the big league. Preparations for the most ordinary birthday party take on the tension of a moonshot countdown. The mum who lets herself in for a children's party shares with astronauts a special blend of domestic patriotism and controlled panic. When the party's over, and she shuts the door behind the last small guest, we're the first to offer our highest award for courage and endurance. (We hope her own child got a balloon, too.)

Why do mums give children's parties? A great many, very sensibly, don't. Birthday celebrations, yes; birthday cakes, by all means; parties, never. Some mothers hold birthdays to family only and set up the tradition. Others try a party once, take a vow of abstinence and accept a feeling of guilt as their due penance for letting the kids go on accepting invitations. A lot of mums bake a cake, tell the birthday child to ask a couple of mates round for the afternoon, lay out crisps and juice and call it a day. One mother cleared her conscience about her children's social obligations by giving a marathon picnic one Sunday. She monitored the weather forecasts and included all the parents too. Everyone had a good time and of course the parents all helped.

But this chapter is for those who, either by accident or design, find themselves having to give a party for a child of any age between three and eleven-plus. We hope that at this point a majority of mothers can heave a thankful sigh that they got out from under in time, or that children's parties have never caught on in their neighbourhood (the infection spreads from one household to another like dry rot). Anyone who just needs ideas for novelty birthday cakes should look up the relevant age-group and ignore everything else in the section.

There's no doubt that a birthday is B-Day, *the* day, and a birthday cake underlines the point. Every child we asked about parties had birthday cake top of the priority list. Turn to pages 97-98 for the basic cake and icing recipes and refer back to these for any particular cake we suggest. The basic cake and all its variations work – we emphasize that it's how they *look*, not how they taste, that matters. Don't bother to make the cake yourself if you don't feel like it: just buy one to the necessary shape and size and decorate according to the child's fancy or to one of our suggestions. They're all easy; they're all fun; kids are knocked out by them.

For once, the ever-changing tastes of growing kids are a help. The age-groups and food preferences break down clearly. And it should go without saying that any of us would be crazy to spend more than we can afford on a party for any age-group. The whole point of a party, and party food for children, is *effect*. Up to the age of about eight they're not primarily interested in eating at parties. Over the age of eight they will eat almost anything savoury set before them and will probably hurl the sweet goodies at each other and at the ceiling. Over the age of eleven children display a deceptively sophisticated facade, but in fact are as conservative about food as any three-year-old. (Parties for this age-group mainly concern girls: eleven-plus boys will seldom allow themselves to be caught, dead or alive, at anything labelled 'party'.) Don't overdo either the variety of food or the effort you put into it. The keynotes are colour, imagination, and knowing what the kids really want at a particular age. Anything else is to please *you*, or a waste of time and money, depending on how you look at it.

All the suggestions given here have been tested, proved popular, and are too good to leave out of a comprehensive list of party food. *Select.* Don't use any more of them than you're sure you need, unless you want to fill your cake and biscuit tins for the next month or so.

Before going through the four age-groups blow by candle blow, here's the basic birthday cake recipe and the icings that go with it. It's the standard success story up to the age of eleven.

### Basic birthday sponge cake

100 g (4 oz) soft margarine
100 g (4 oz) self-raising flour
1 teaspoon baking powder
100 g (4 oz) sugar
2 eggs
1 tablespoon milk

*Flavouring*
Orange/Lemon – a drop or two of orange or lemon essence *or* a dessertspoon of grated orange or lemon rind
Vanilla – add a drop or two of vanilla essence
Chocolate – add a tablespoon of cocoa or chocolate powder to the flour

Put the marge, flour, baking powder, sugar, eggs, and milk into a bowl with the chosen flavouring and mix everything together like mad for 2 minutes. (Or whirl for 30 seconds in an electric mixer.)

Bake in the types of tin and to the times specified for the novelty cakes. These vary: the basic sponge doesn't. Remember to grease each tin and, preferably, to line it with oiled greaseproof paper too, so the finished sponge will turn out well. These ingredients are plenty for 8 children. Double up for a larger party and for the occasional novelty cake which should be larger to look right.

You'll need one, or the other, and sometimes both kinds of basic icing for the cakes:

**Glacé icing**

250 g (8 oz) sifted icing sugar
2 tablespoons (approximately) hot water

Double or treble these amounts as required for the cakes. Beat the water into the icing sugar a drop at a time until the mixture thickly coats the back of a wooden spoon. Glacé icing hardens pretty fast so make it, with a drop or two of food colouring if required, just before you need it and it will be easy to spread. It hardens to a smooth, shiny finish.

**Butter icing**

100 g (4 oz) sifted icing sugar
50 g (2 oz) soft margarine or butter
a few drops of milk

Double or treble these amounts as you need and add food colouring as required. Cream the marge and sugar together until pale and fluffy, with only as much milk as you need to make it easy to spread.

To help cut the trickier cake designs you will need to make a paper pattern. The easiest way is to fold the paper in half lengthwise and draw the shape of half the design. Then cut round the pattern, open up the paper and use it to shape the cake (which will at least be symmetrical). You can keep the pattern in place on the cake with cocktail sticks. The scraps of sponge left over after cutting out a design make a good base for a trifle.

The only other item required for birthday cake making is a tray, board, or something similarly flat to serve the finished cake on. Plates, however large, aren't flat enough.

And that's all the basic equipment. Now for the kids, their parties, and the food.

## THE UNDER-FIVES

The catch about little children's parties is that the kids often bring their mothers, which can mean a lady-like tea as well as refereeing the bunfight. Keep all food very simple and rely on the birthday cake, colour, and decorations to pull you through. Mothers of under-fives need all their health and strength because most of this age-group behave abominably at their birthday parties as a result of becoming over-excited, over-indulged, and over-tired. By the time the party is due to start, mothers are ready to scream – but we can't because it's his day and he'll get worse if we do. The small guests are quite likely to behave badly too: it's hard on them to see one child getting all the limelight. Some mothers harden their hearts and put NPP (no presents, please) on the party invitations, but if the children do bring presents you can sidestep trouble by snatching them at the door and hiding them all until the party is over. Then the birthday child can have a private orgy of unwrapping while his mother has a drink with her feet up. If presents are opened on the spot there's always that one little guest who bursts into tears and wants to keep what he brought.

Get lots of balloons ready – two per child at least. If you hand each child a balloon as he arrives he will have something to play with while the rest are trickling in, and so may not change his mind about coming and want to go home. Another way to keep small children occupied until you can start jolly games is to have a few colouring books and crayons laid out in a corner; leave them scattered casually and steer a shy child over to them if necessary. But under-fives usually arrive bang on time – and one or two may even come early. Some children get so excited that they can't wait.

Mothers should be discouraged: this is a kids' party, not theirs. If mothers come too, you'll have to clean the house and put on a decent dress instead of letting the house go hang until afterwards and wearing jeans. If one or two mothers do stay, make them work. And the best way to get rid of a mother who is hovering on the doorstep is to offer, as if it were the chance of a lifetime, to let *her* organize the games.

If possible, arrange to deliver the children home yourself after the party, instead of waiting for them to be collected. All you do is shout 'The party's over!' and rush them into their coats. If the kids are being collected from your house, you'll feel obliged to dig out the sherry when the parents return to exclaim over your efforts and declare that they could never give such a wonderful party. If you must offer them anything, try a harassed look and a mangled piece of birthday cake.

*Always have tea early on.* Two or three games before tea is plenty. Small children won't care much about eating tea, but they know it's there, they're excited, and time will hang heavy on everybody's hands until they see the cake and start spilling the lemonade. If it's a 3 o'clock kick-off you can figure on having tea at 3-30. The major games and entertainment should come after tea and will be much less stressful for having got tea over and the ice broken. If you're lucky you may find that the kids are happy merely to play (or race around shrieking and yelling) after tea, so that you don't need to use your carefully devised amusements. So much the better. Now here's a selection of party food.

## NOVELTY CAKES FOR THE UNDER FIVES

### Elephant cake

A real charmer: easy, cheap, and showy. Mix the basic sponge ingredients (page 97) and divide between 2 round cake tins about 18 cm (7 in.) in diameter. Bake at 325°F (170°C or gas 3-4) for 25-35 minutes, then turn out on to a wire rack and cool.

Put one round on a flat tray or board to form the elephant's body. Then cut a smaller round out of the centre of the other, using a small plate or saucer to cut round, leaving a 2·5 cm-

wide (1 in.) border edge. Cut a small scoop out of this smaller round to fit it as a head to the body. Now divide the remaining border into 3: 1 piece for the elephant's trunk and cut the other 2 pieces in half to make 4 legs.

Make butter icing with 250 g (8 oz) icing sugar and 100 g (4 oz) marge, and colour it shocking pink with food colouring. Stick the pieces of the elephant's anatomy to the body with a dab of icing; then ice over the whole elephant.

Cut a stick of black liquorice into strips and use a loop for the elephant's ear, a small circle for his eye, a thicker piece for his tusk and one for his tail. If there's any left over, cut it into little bits for toenails. And that's all. Having got the basic sponge and icing ready, the actual art work takes 10 minutes. The elephant can be any colour you like, but pink looks wonderful.

**Man-in-the-moon cake**

Double the sponge ingredients (page 97) for this one and bake in a round tin about 25 cm (10 in.) in diameter at 325°F (170°C or gas 3-4) for 45-50 minutes. Turn out and cool.

Draw a man-in-the-moon crescent shape (you'll find this in an illustrated book of nursery rhymes) on a round of paper the same size as the cake tin. Cut this out and use it as a pattern to cut the sponge, securing it with toothpicks if necessary. Leave the shape on the wire rack while you make glacé icing and colour it yellow; then put a plate under the

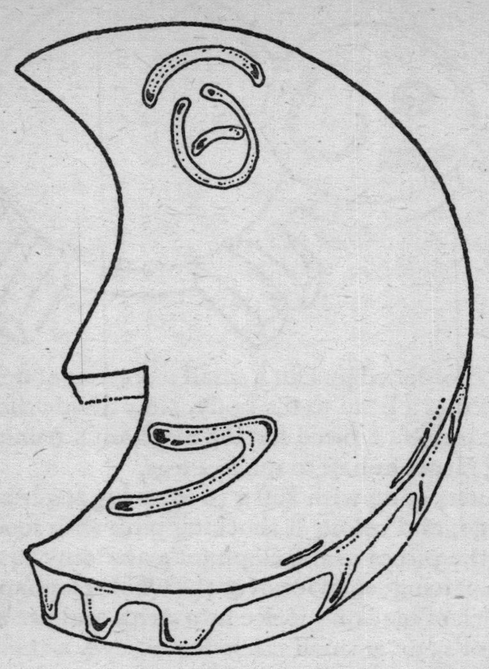

rack to catch the drips and pour the icing over the cake, smoothing it carefully all over. When the glacé icing has set, lift the cake on to the serving tray or cake board.

Make a little bit of butter icing with 50 g (2 oz) icing sugar and 25 g (1 oz) marge, and colour it brown with chocolate powder. Dig out the set of piping tube and nozzles which has been lying at the back of the kitchen drawer since your wedding (if you haven't got a set, get one: plastic is all right but metal lasts longer and when you discover how easy piping is you might get quite keen – but *don't* struggle with big icing bags which only experts can handle). Smear the brown butter icing into the tube, screw on a nozzle and pipe an eye and a big smile on to the cake. The tray will have added appeal if you put a toy cow on one side and a little dish and spoon on the other. Then the kids can sing Hey Diddle Diddle as well as Happy Birthday.

### Teddy bear cake

Bake the basic cake mixture (see page 97) in a rectangular cake tin or Swiss roll tin, about 30 cm × 20 cm (12 in. × 8 in.) for 25-30 minutes at 325°F (170°C or gas 3-4). Turn out and cool on a wire rack.

Draw a teddy bear shape on a piece of paper the same size as your tin and cut round the cake using this pattern (see page 98 for pattern making). Make yellow glacé icing as for Man-in-the-moon (page 98) and ice the teddy all over. Use chocolate drops or any little coloured sweets for his eyes and some buttons down his front; and use a little strip of liquorice for his nose and mouth.

If you're really in a creative frame of mind you could make a 'present' from the left-over sponge trimmings tied with liquorice 'string'. Icing will stick loose pieces together and will hide any cracks. Put the 'present' under the teddy's paw.

**Railway cake**

Almost any size or shape of sponge cake, bought or home-made, will do for this one. What's on top is what matters.

Glacé ice the cake (375 g or 12 oz icing sugar) all over in plain white or grass-green. Now put some glacé icing in a contrasting colour (deep blue is good) into your piping tube, screw on a fine nozzle and pipe a double line of railway tracks around the edge of the cake or zig-zagging over the top. If thin-line piping is a weak point, thin strips of liquorice will do for the rails and also for the sleepers in between. Use little bits of coloured paper stuck onto cocktail sticks for signals. You can make a tunnel by rolling out a piece of marzipan (buy this ready-made in slabs) about $\frac{1}{2}$ cm ($\frac{1}{4}$ in.) thick, cutting a piece and moulding it into the right shape over the rails. Finally borrow a small toy engine and place it in position.

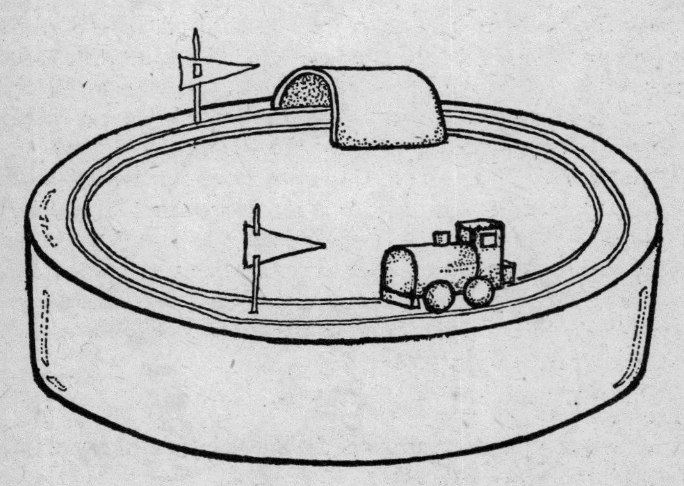

**Humpty Dumpty cake**

This is a good idea for an Easter party or for a child whose birthday falls about that time, when chocolate eggs are available.

Bake the basic sponge mixture in a loaf tin for about 45 minutes at 325°F (170°C or gas 3-4). Make some white glacé icing (using 375 g or 12 oz icing sugar; see page 98 for method) and use most of it to ice the 'wall' all over. When it has set, lift the cake on to a flat tray or board.

Thin the rest of the glacé icing with a drop or two of water if it seems to need it, and colour it red or orange. Pipe this in thin lines across the wall, criss-crossing at intervals to resemble bricks. Now pipe 2 eyes and a smile on to a chocolate egg. Scoop out a deep hollow on top of the 'wall' and secure the egg here with a little icing, so that Humpty looks as if he were sitting on a wall.

**Train cake**

Buy a Swiss roll, a packet of ready-made marzipan and 50 g (2 oz) of plain dark chocolate.

Make butter icing with 250 g (8 oz) icing sugar and 100 g (4 oz) marge and mix in the melted chocolate: it will go rather runny but will harden on the cake. Place the Swiss roll on a tray or board and carefully ice the cake all over.

Knead the marzipan with a drop or two of red food colouring and roll it out $\frac{1}{2}$ cm ($\frac{1}{4}$ in.) thick. Cut 4 circles about 2·5 cm (1 in.) in diameter for the train wheels; and roll a piece of marzipan for the funnel. Position these on the cake, make a face on one end of the train with a few little coloured sweets, and twist a pipe-cleaner or liquorice to stick into the funnel for smoke.

This is enough for 8 children, and 8 is enough for any party unless you're going wild. If you go wild, buy more Swiss rolls, double up the icing and make a string of carriages for the train.

**Number cake**

Buy or borrow a cake tin in the shape of the numeral you want, or draw the number on paper and cut out a cake to fit. Glacé ice or butter ice all over in a pretty colour. Apart from the candles, there's no need for any more decoration.

Small children love this idea; and of course learn instantly and forever what a 3 or a 4 looks like.

### Individual birthday cakes

If you're making a birthday cake for a party, it's a tactful thought to double up the basic sponge recipe and bake half of it in a separate tin to be cut into individual iced squares, one for each child. Pipe the children's names on them if you feel like using them as place-cakes. Smaller kids probably won't eat them, but they'll like having their own candles to blow out at the magic moment.

## PARTY FOOD FOR THE UNDER-FIVES

Here is an extravagant list of suggestions from which you need only select one or two. Always hold back on sweet things in preference to savoury. There's nothing like chocolate for spoiling pretty party clothes, and if the kids do show interest in anything sweet, let it be the birthday cake. *Cut all items to bite-size.* This age-group likes to take a bite here and a bite there and you'll wind up with a mound of half-eaten sandwiches if you cut them normally.

### Ribbon sandwiches

Trim slices of brown and white bread to equal size and sandwich them together for a chequered effect: brown-white and white-brown. Fill them with your children's own favourites or with one or two of the following fillings, and cut them into ribbon strips or tiny squares. You can make the bread slices thinner if you roll them lightly with a rolling pin first.

*Fillings*

Meat paste mixed with a little scrambled egg
Banana mashed with a drip of honey and a drop of lemon juice
Cream cheese mixed with chopped peanuts
Cottage or cream cheese mixed with marmalade

### Savouries

Potato crisps or sticks; cocktail sausages on coloured sticks; buttered popcorn.

## Gingerbread men

If your nerves can stand it you could let the children help make their ginger army.

250 g (½ lb) plain flour
100 g (¼ lb) margarine
100 g (¼ lb) soft brown sugar
1 teaspoon ground ginger
1 tablespoon orange juice or orange marmalade
1 tablespoon black treacle
1 tablespoon golden syrup
currants for buttons

Mix all these ingredients together and then roll out the mixture on a floured board. Using a small gingerbread man cutter, cut out about 20 little men. Now everyone can help to decorate the shapes with currant buttons.

Bake for 10 to 12 minutes at 350°F (180°C, gas 4). When you take them out of the oven they seem alarmingly soft, but as they cool they become crisp.

## Haystacks

Melt a few ounces of cooking chocolate with a knob of butter in a basin over hot water. Stir in cornflakes or rice crispies until the liquid is absorbed and the mixture fairly stiff. Put teaspoons of this into tiny paper cases and chill to set.

## Chocolate marshmallows

Melt cooking chocolate in a basin over hot water and put a dessertspoonful into tiny paper cases. Press pink and white marshmallows on top of the chocolate before it sets.

## Truffles

Melt a 250 g (8 oz) plain dark slab of chocolate in a basin over hot water and stir in a good tablespoonful of condensed milk. Beat well, then leave to cool until it is stiff. Form into small balls, dip in condensed milk and roll each one in chocolate vermicelli or coloured sugar strands. Park them in small paper cases.

## Chocolate cream fingers

This recipe and the next one are less simple to make, but go down very well with any older children or mothers who have stayed for the party. They fall into a category graphically described by a dieting mum as 'a moment on the lips – a lifetime on the hips'.

50 g (2 oz) icing sugar
100 g (4 oz) marge
1 egg
100 g (4 oz) cornflour
100 g (4 oz) plain flour

Cream the fat with the sugar until light and fluffy, then beat in the egg. Sift in the two kinds of flour and mix to a stiff dough. Roll teaspoonfuls of this mixture into sausage shapes, lay them on a greased baking sheet and press each one down with a fork. Bake at 325°F (170°C or gas 3-4) for 20 minutes, and allow to cool.

Sandwich together in twos with butter icing, using 100 g (4 oz) sugar and 50 g (2 oz) marge. Finally melt 50 g (2 oz) plain dark chocolate in a basin over hot water and dip the ends of the fingers into it. Chill to set.

**Baby éclairs**

50 g (2 oz) butter or marge
125 ml (5 fl oz or ¼ pint) water
a pinch of salt
75 g (3 oz) plain flour
2 large eggs
whipped double cream for filling

*Icing*
50 g (2 oz) plain chocolate
1 tablespoon water
1 tablespoon milk
100 g (4 oz) icing sugar

Bring the fat, water, and salt to the boil in a pan. Add the flour, take the pan off the heat and beat until smooth. Let the mixture cool, then beat in the eggs one at a time. Drop teaspoons of this mixture on to a greased baking sheet and bake at 425°F (220°C or gas 7) for 25-30 minutes. Take out and cool for a minute or two, then cut a slit in each one. Fill with whipped cream when quite cool.

Make chocolate icing by melting 50 g (2 oz) plain chocolate with a tablespoon of water and a tablespoon of milk in a basin over hot water; then add 100 g (4 oz) sifted icing sugar and beat well. Brush on the chocolate icing with a pastry brush or, if you have the nerve, dip each top into the icing mixture.

Chill to set. (When adults meet these at parties they call them profiteroles.)

**Orange oo-la-la**

A glob of ice-cream per child is the traditional way of ending a party tea for young children. Here are a couple of good alternatives.

Cut oranges in half and scoop out the pulp. Fill the halves with orange jelly and let it set – you can chop the pulp, drain it and mix it into the jelly if you like, or save it for fruit salad next day.

When the jelly is firm, cut the orange halves into quarters and serve. They look pretty and kids love them.

**Toadstools in jelly**

Make up a green jelly and pour it into a large shallow dish. When it is just setting, cut bananas in half and place one half per child standing upright in the jelly. Lay a meringue shell over each 'stalk', and dot each shell with whipped cream spiked with red food colouring.

And after all this fuss and all this food, it is still important to remember that children may not be interested in it except as a spectacle. If you want them to eat, there is nothing to beat an individual box of small items for each child: a packet of crisps, a bottle of lemonade, a straw, and a packet of little sweets can be as exciting as the most glamorous party tea.

From the children's viewpoint the party becomes *their* special occasion as well as the birthday child's.

And if you want them to have a good time, there is nothing to beat *crackers*. Crackers are hard to get at any time except Christmas; they are expensive; they are the most exciting kind of treat. A box or two of crackers stored away against a children's party is a mother's version of laying up treasure in heaven.

## THE FIVE-TO-EIGHTS

This age-group represents the real hard core of party-goers. These kids know it all: they criticize the food, the games, the presents; they shout, roar, and go wild at the drop of a balloon. They will also enjoy themselves tremendously if they know who's boss. There is no excuse at all for other mothers to stay, so you can feel free to boss if you have to.

All the suggestions given for party food for the under-fives still apply. The five-to-eights will take more interest in the food – not much, but some – with even greater emphasis on savouries. Sweet things are liable to end up on the floor. The birthday cake is still the star of the show, but don't count on the children to eat more than a mouthful: this crowd wants large quantities of crisps and fizzy drinks and wants above all to be allowed to make a noise.

It's an unfortunate truth that school friends and 'others' rarely mix. 'Others' feel isolated, often get treated as if they had B.O., and can have a lonely afternoon. They just don't know the language of school, that's all, and the older the child the more important school friends become.

## NOVELTY CAKES FOR THE FIVE-TO-EIGHTS

(See page 97-98 for basic cake and icing recipes)

### Army Football Cowboy cake

Make and bake the basic cake mixture in a rectangular cake tin, 30 cm × 20 cm (12 in. × 8 in.), at 325°F (170°C or gas 3-4) for 25-30 minutes. Turn on to a wire rack and cool.

Make glacé icing (page 98) using 250 g (8 oz) icing sugar,

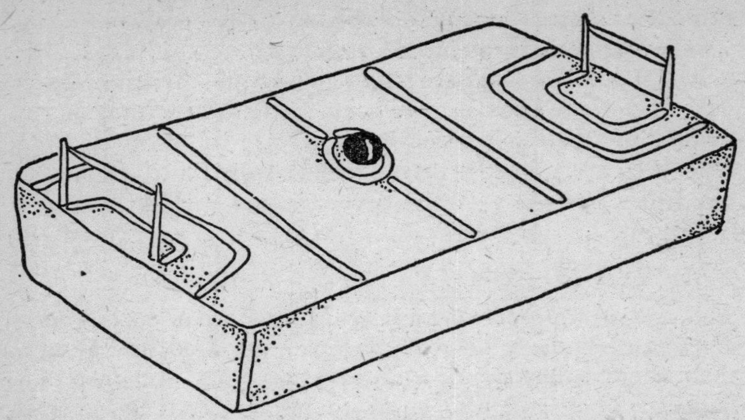

colour it green and ice the cake all over. Before it sets, position any available selection of toy soldiers and tiny cannon, and stick little flags made with coloured paper and toothpicks around the edge, between the birthday candles.

This idea has a lot of variations: *Cowboys and Indians* on a yellow icing; *Zoo* animals in little enclosures made from halved toothpicks; *Racing cars* lined up on piped icing tracks beside a little chequered flag; a *Show jumping arena* with jumps and fences and tiny horses parading around the edge; a *Football pitch* with markings piped in white glacé icing on a green ground, toothpick goalposts, and a little coloured ball in the middle (see Truffles, page 108).

They're all easy to do and are good for mixed parties and boys-only. Girls-only prefer:

**House cake**

Bake the basic sponge mixture in 2 square cake tins about 18 cm (7 in.) square, at 325°F (170°C or gas 3-4) for 25-30 minutes. Turn on to a wire rack and cool.

Ice one of the squares with white glacé icing for the 'house' using 250 g (8 oz) icing sugar. Using a paper pattern, cut a 'roof' shape from the other square and cut a chimney or two from the trimmings. Lay the iced square on a tray or board and join the other pieces to it with a little jam.

Make coloured butter icing using 250 g (8 oz) icing sugar, 100 g (4 oz) marge, and ice over the roof and chimney. Ice a little door on to the house, and pipe window outlines with the rest of the butter icing. Stick a twist of liquorice in the chimney for smoke.

**Doll cake**

Refer back to the Teddy bear cake on page 103, and cut a paper pattern in the shape of a doll instead (check back for making cake patterns, page 98). Cut round the sponge, then glacé ice all over in white or pink or brown, using 250 g (8 oz) icing sugar. Make butter icing with 250 g (8 oz) icing

sugar and 100 g (4 oz) marge and divide it. Colour one lot and use it for the doll's hair; colour the other for the dress and shoes. Finally pipe features on the face if you can manage the twiddles.

## PARTY FOOD FOR THE FIVE-TO-EIGHTS

**Ribbon sandwiches** (page 107) are very popular, if only to look at. Cut into ribbon strips, or into squares laid out like a chequer-board. Any of the fillings suggested for the under-fives go down well, or you can move on to the following:

*Fillings*

Finely chopped ham mixed into cream cheese
Tomato, mashed and flavoured with a little finely chopped onion
Cottage or cream cheese mixed with well-drained sweetcorn
Tuna fish mashed with salad cream

## Savouries

Potato crisps and sticks; cocktail sausages or small frankfurters on coloured sticks. A good way to serve sausages is to scoop out the inside of a round cottage loaf and put the hot sausages in the hollow – this will keep warm in the oven and the loaf helps to soak up excess fat.

## Sandwich platter

Stamp circles out of thick slices of brown and white bread with a pastry cutter. Make these into open sandwiches, using your own or some of these toppings:

Sardines mashed with shredded lettuce, garnished with a slice of cucumber
Finely chopped chicken garnished with a slice of tomato
Seasoned hard-boiled egg on overlapping cucumber slices
Banana mashed with a little sugar and lemon juice, garnished with grated chocolate and a banana slice

## Sweet biscuits and buns

See Under-fives section, and expect the five-to-eights to use them as missiles rather than eat them. But they'll enjoy Traffic lights.

## Traffic light biscuits

These are fiddly but fun. Make a shortbread biscuit mixture as follows:

100 g (4 oz) margarine
50 g (2 oz) caster sugar
125 g (5 oz) plain flour
25 g (1 oz) cornflour

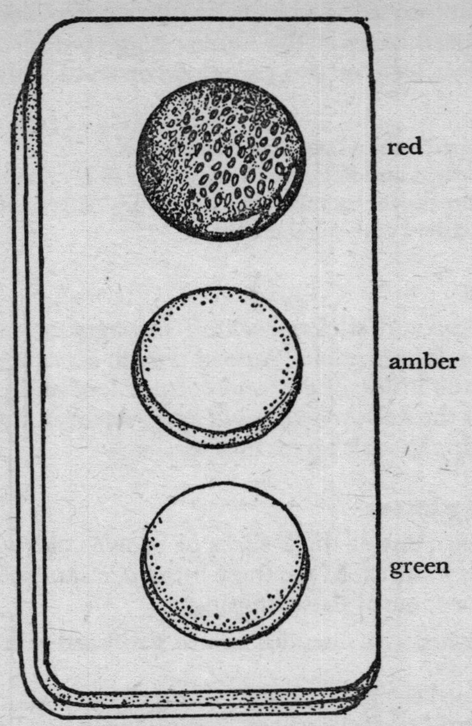


Cream the marge and sugar and add the flours sieved together. Knead the mixture gently on a floured board. Now roll it out and cut into strips about 8 cm (3 in.) long and 2 cm (1 in.) wide. Lay half the strips on a baking sheet. Now, using an apple corer or something equally small as a cutter, carefully stamp three little discs out of each of the remaining strips so the holes look like the vertical tier of traffic lights. Re-roll the discs and the other trimmings and repeat as long as you and the mixture hold out.

Bake both the plain and the cut-out strips at 350°F (180°C or gas 4) for about 15 minutes. When they are cooked and cooled, smear one side of each strip all over with icing, or ice-cream sauce from a tube, or plain jam. Place each cut out strip on top of each plain strip like a sandwich.

Now fill in the holes. The simplest way of all is to use coloured sweeties, but you can also try jams – gooseberry jam or anything suitably green at the bottom, strawberry for the top and lemon curd or marmalade in the middle. If you haven't got the right colour you can spike stiff pale honey with bright food colouring.

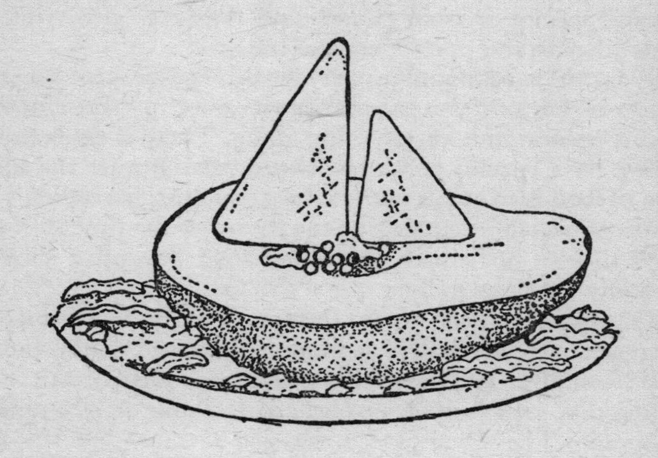

**Sailing boats** (for 8)

500 ml (1 pint) green jelly
4 small pears
1 small carton (125 ml or 5 fl oz) double cream
8 ice-cream wafers

Pour the made-up jelly into a bowl and let it set. Then chop it into pieces with a knife and whisk well to break it up completely. Divide the jelly mixture between eight saucers.

Peel the pears, cut them in half and scoop out the cores with a teaspoon. Put an upturned pear-half on the jelly in each saucer. Whip the cream stiff and pipe lines of cream to look like 'waves' on the jelly 'sea'. Cut each wafer into one small and one larger triangle and press these into each pear half for 'sails', using a little cream to fix them firmly. Add a few tiny sweets or silver sugar balls to each core hollow for 'treasure'.

## THE EIGHT-TO-ELEVENS

Mums who learned the hard way lay emphasis on the difficulties of mixing both boys and girls at this age. Outdoor parties in the summer, when the kids can wear relaxing and familiar clothes and play Hare-and-Hounds stand more chance of success than indoor parties with organized progressive games or card games, and the sexes glowering at each other from opposite ends of the room.

By far the most popular party for this age-group – and the five-to-eights too if you can manage it – is a trip to the cinema, circus, pantomime, or anything going. There is no point in laying on a special party tea afterwards because the kids' idea of food is to eat as many crisps, peanuts, ice lollies, and ice-creams as they can during the show; by the time they get back they're not concerned about food beyond a slice of birthday cake and gallons of soft drinks.

Transport is a problem for this sort of party, but if you can arrange it, it's worth it. One mother borrowed a mini-bus to take 17 children to a Disney double feature. Others wait until fathers and, hopefully, transport are available on a Saturday afternoon. The advantage is that *you* can decide when the party is over and deliver the children back yourself. This can save a lot of wear and tear on both parents and premises.

If the party is at home and you're doing a party tea, all the suggestions for the previous age-groups still stand. Food preferences are the same, only more so: the child who will eat a whole plate of tomato sandwiches and drink 6 glasses of Coke is by no means unusual.

Party or not, the birthday cake is still first in importance. Refer back to the five-to-eights for a comprehensive list of novelties, and here are 3 rather more sophisticated ideas.

## NOVELTY CAKES FOR THE EIGHT-TO-ELEVENS

(See page 97-98 for basic sponge and icing recipes.)

### Guitar cake

Double the quantities given for the basic sponge cake and bake the mixture divided between two rectangular tins, or

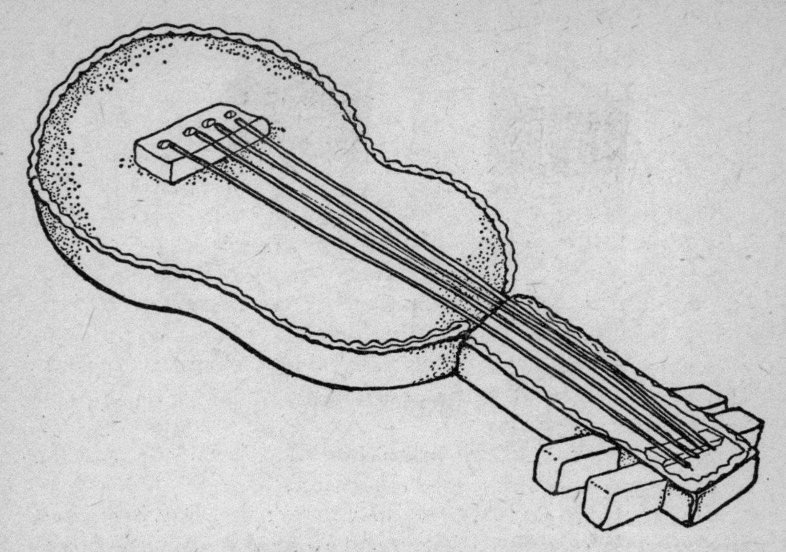

Swiss roll tins, about 30 cm × 20 cm (12 in. × 8 in.) at 325°F (170°C or gas 3-4) for 25-30 minutes. You'll also need 3 packets of ready-made marzipan and a few sticks of liquorice and some jam.

Cut a piece of paper the same size as the tin, fold it lengthwise and draw the shape of half a guitar without its handle piece. Cut round this pattern, open up the paper and use it to shape one of the cakes. Cut a 7·5 cm (3 in.) wide strip from the other sponge to form the handle piece. Place the two parts of the guitar on a large tray and glue them together with a little jam.

Now roll out the marzipan and cut the *complete* guitar shape from it, using the same paper pattern, and adding the handle as well. Cut small pieces shaped as guitar 'keys' and 'string pegs'. Smear the surface of the cake with melted jam and stick the marzipan into position. Finally press on the musical bits and cut long thin strips of liquorice to lay on the guitar for 'strings'. If you enjoy using the icing tube (some mothers do), you can pipe an edging pattern to close the gap between the marzipan top and the sponge cake sides.

**Record cake**

Bake the basic sponge (page 97) in a 23 cm (9 in.) cake tin at 325°F (170°C or gas 3-4) for 35 minutes.

Make chocolate butter icing with 250 g (8 oz) sifted icing sugar, 100 g (4 oz) soft marge and 75 g (3 oz) melted dark chocolate. You'll also need a packet of marzipan.

When the sponge is cool, place it on a tray or cake board. Smooth most of the icing over the cake, reserving a little for your piping tube.

Mark the icing on the cake with a fork to represent record 'grooves'. Roll out the marzipan and cut a circle 7·5 cm (3 in.) in diameter. Punch a small hole in the centre of the marzipan circle. Lay it on the middle of the cake and pipe on the name of a favourite pop star or current hit, using the rest of the butter icing.

**Card cake**

Any card in the pack will do, but diamonds are easiest to copy and red is more festive than black. The Ace, or the number corresponding to the child's age, are both good.

Bake the basic sponge in a rectangular tin at 325°F (170°C or gas 3-4) for 25-35 minutes. Make white glacé icing using

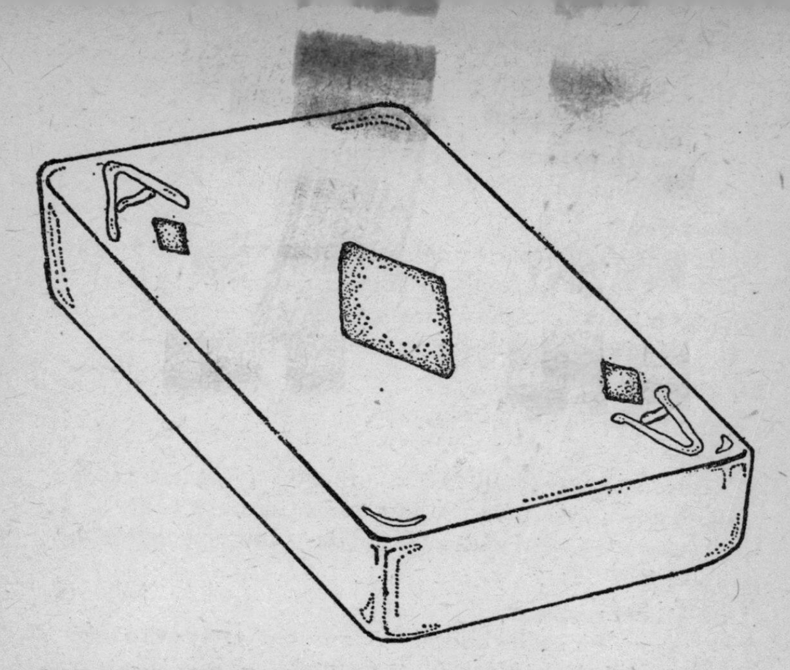

250 g (8 oz) sifted icing sugar and about 2 tablespoons of hot water. Make some butter icing too, using 100 g (4 oz) sifted icing sugar creamed with 50 g (2 oz) soft margarine, and colour it bright red.

Cool the cake on a wire rack and put a plate underneath to catch the drips. Glacé ice the sponge all over and let it set; then lift it carefully on to a tray or board. Butter ice the red diamond motif in the centre. Pipe an A, or the relevant number, on diagonally opposite corners.

## PARTY FOOD FOR THE EIGHT-TO-ELEVENS

### Sandwiches

Refer back to Ribbon sandwiches and their fillings on pages 107 and 114. Cut into fingers or squares.

### Rolls

Use a filling suggestion or two to cover split rolls: egg, ham, tomato, tuna, and cheese-and-nut are all popular.

**Savouries**
Crisps, popcorn, sausages or sausage rolls, hot dogs; maybe even hamburgers.

**Sweet things**
Refer back to Chocolate fingers and Baby éclairs on pages 108-109. Otherwise small meringues filled with coloured cream, or fruit-filled pastry tarts, or brandy snaps. The eight-to-elevens are still savoury-minded, not sweet.

**Drinks**
Fizzy lemonade, Coca Cola, etc.

**Extras**
Toadstools in jelly (page 110) or orange jelly quarters (page 110) go down well. So do Sailing boats (see page 117). Otherwise ice-cream with a chocolate or butterscotch sauce (see pages 51-52).

**Highly recommended**
A picnic box for each child, for an outdoor party or to take to a show. Make the kids collect their rubbish in it afterwards for disposal.
Children in this age-group eat more, but are impressed by quantity, rather than variety of choice. Go easy on sweet goodies; and don't forget drinking straws at each and every party.

## ELEVEN-PLUS

Eleven-plus signals all change for adolescence: mothers brace themselves. Suddenly the kids want to be treated like adults, but while they enjoy the idea they are unnerved by the reality. Parties for this age-group reflect changing tastes and attitudes and require the utmost in domestic diplomacy. It *is* possible to have a mixed party, but it's not easy; an outdoor bonfire party, a firework party, and a barbecue with team games have all been known to work, but not without the fire-and-spark risks involved and a very firm hand from dad as well as mum.

The ideal party for eleven-plus girls is an early-evening movie with selected bosom friends, then home for a buffet supper which looks very sophisticated but in fact runs along simple and conservative lines. Birthday cake has to be called 'gâteau' – but it still has to be there.

Sandwiches are scorned as kids' stuff: crisps and cheese biscuits to dunk in dips are fine. Balloons, squeakers, and blowers go out of the window: candles around the room create the kind of atmosphere the kids want. Food means a fork supper – they may be reluctant to sit round a table.

Here is a good and easy recipe for a chocolate cake which can be split into several layers and prettied up to look as glamorous as their heart's desire. They can eat it with forks, and it makes a good pudding as well as being the birthday cake they secretly want.

**Chocolate gâteau**

4 eggs
100 g (4 oz) caster sugar
75 g (3 oz) self-raising flour
25 g (1 oz) cocoa powder
3 tablespoons corn oil

*Icing:*
500 g (1 lb) sifted icing sugar
250 g (8 oz) marge or butter
6 tablespoons cocoa powder
1 tablespoon instant coffee powder
4 tablespoons hot water

Whisk the eggs with the sugar until the mixture is light and creamy and the whisk leaves a trail behind it when lifted out. Sift the flour and cocoa powder together and fold them in; then gently fold in the oil. Grease and line a deep cake tin about 20 cm (8 in.) in diameter, pour in the cake mixture, and bake at 350°F (180°C or gas 4) for about 45 minutes.

Turn out and cool on a wire rack; let it go cold before splitting it into four rounds.

Make chocolate butter icing using 500 g (1 lb) sifted icing sugar creamed with 250 g (8 oz) soft marge or butter. Mix 6 tablespoons of cocoa powder and 1 tablespoonful coffee powder with 4 tablespoons of hot water, and stir this into the icing.

Sandwich the cake rounds together with part of the icing; then ice the sides and roll them in chocolate vermicelli. Finally coat the top of the cake with icing and decorate with silver sugar balls or something the kids will not look sideways at. (Make cautious enquiries before adding any birthday candles.)

It is a snare and a delusion to suppose that the eleven-plus age-group will like unusual or even interesting party food. They don't. They like chicken casserole with boiled rice. Even a mild curry is too risky, and goulash can scare them stiff. If a proper hot dish isn't called for, they'll be happy with sausage rolls or vol-au-vents filled with sardine, chicken, tuna, mushroom, or scrambled egg. They like Knickerbocker Glories in tall glasses with brightly coloured plastic spoons; and they like coloured paper napkins laboriously folded into fancy shapes.

Here's the Chicken casserole, and the Knickerbocker Glory:

**Chicken casserole** (for 8-10)

1 large or two medium chickens
2 sliced onions
3 or 4 sliced carrots
seasoning (plus a bouquet garni if you have one)

Simmer the whole chicken for about an hour with the other ingredients in a large pan with water to cover. Take it out when it is tender and strain the stock into a bowl. When the chicken is cool, discard the skin and as much of the fat as possible; then take the flesh off the bones and chop into pieces. (Put the bones and carcass back into the stock to boil up for soup another day.)

Make a sauce with 75 g (3 oz) marge, 75 g (3 oz) flour and 750 ml (1½ pints) milk or milk-and-stock. Check for seasoning, then mix in the chicken pieces and put the whole lot into a casserole or overproof dish.

Heat it up slowly when you need it, and serve with boiled rice mixed with green peas and sweet corn. And crisps.

**Knickerbocker glory**

Put layers of jelly, custard, sponge cake, and fruit into tall glasses as if you were making a trifle. Top with a swirl of whipped cream and a cherry. Chill well and serve with long spoons.

Eleven-plus boys like this sort of food too, but the setting should be much more casual – they tend to be suspicious of glamour. Dainty dips won't do. Hot dogs, hamburgers, or a cold meat platter with baked potatoes do very well.

A father we know, asked for an opinion on kids' parties in general, and eleven-plus parties in particular, didn't hesitate. A party, he said, is letting the kids do what they're not allowed to do at any other time – playing in the coalhole, making a racket, staying up late, talking with their mouths full and laughing like hyenas at absurd jokes. Mothers glumly call this Children's Lib.

# 7 Problems

Problems here mean the kind you ring your best friend about. The kind your mother-in-law might ring her best friend about. The kind worth clucking over, but not worth sitting in a surgery for. You shouldn't need a doctor to deal with most of them, but many a minor feeding problem can seem just as serious as a clinical one like projectile vomiting or an allergy to eggs.

Most of us learn the difference between medical and non-medical feeding difficulties during the first year of the first baby. We take the L-plates off the pram on the day we realize that spitting back the carrots is a gesture of defiance, not the first sign of twisted intestine. But from then on it's a long haul, with problems flourishing like weeds all the way.

The fussy, faddy child; the fat child; the frail child; the child mad for sweets; these are the most obvious, the most common feeding problems, and the ones that interest us here. Any child at any time can turn into one of these, and any mother can count on having to cope with one or another of them sooner or later. There are usually good reasons for them, and none need become important if we notice in time and act quickly and without fuss. Unrecognized or ignored, though, a minor irritant can develop into a major worry. Before you know where you are you're losing sleep over it and helping to aggravate the situation by getting cross and tense at meals.

Occasional non-cooperation is part of a child's normal development. Playing up mum is part of growing up. Persistent playing up can be avoided if relations between you and the kids are loving, cheerful, and firm. A couple of pointers: the mother who tries too hard to please her family is likely to have trouble at meals, because children know that's when bad behaviour and non-cooperation is going to hurt most. And the mother who pays attention to her family *only* when she's feeding them can expect her children to exploit mealtimes to attract more notice. Either way it's no fun. Either way it's our fault. A balance of the careful and the casual, the middle way of peace and pleasure, is what we're all aiming at. It's not impossible. It just takes a lot of cunning. It means that mothers have to be on their toes every mealtime for years.

Before looking at those problems in detail we'd like to mention a few of the commonest mistakes made by mothers, including ourselves. First, the lack of sensible thinking about sweets. We think sweets are so important that they merit a whole section on their own, and you'll find that at the end of this chapter.

Second, allowing kids to eat, nibble, or pick between meals as a steady habit. Eating between meals is a passport to trouble over food at any age and the cause of much faddiness, fatness, or loss of appetite. A good rule of thumb is to ban nibbling altogether unless, in your judgment, it's really needed.

A third, and very common pitfall is bribery. All the child guidance experts say firmly that we mustn't use sweets, puddings, any kind of treat as a bribe. At the risk of calling down righteous wrath upon our heads, we think it's admissible to stoop to straight bribery if you know what you are doing, recognize the likely consequences and *don't do it often*. Avoid it by all possible means first, and save it for when you need instant co-operation. Overused, bribery backfires badly. It can create a situation where a child will not co-operate about *anything* without a bribe.

Now let's look at those problems.

**Faddy and fussy**

It's fashionable to declare that children have rights like any other section of society, and no one but an ogre would deny that children have the right to dislike certain foods, as any adult has that right. But how do we know when it's a genuine dislike or merely a confidence trick designed to inflate a small ego at the expense of mum's? It's a wise mum who assumes that any dislike is a hoax until proved otherwise.

Faddiness over this, that, and the other food starts in babyhood. It begins to pick up momentum at about two and, if we're lucky, to start easing off around six. It varies wildly, both in terms of the food itself and the child's chosen tactic. And you can count on it being at its worst at the meal you regard as most important.

A typical scenario might go like this. You serve up and the children start eating. Your three-year-old starts to wriggle, then to whine. You ask what's the matter. He doesn't like it. What doesn't he like? That. What? That meat. You bravely say nonsense, it's delicious meat and he ate some only last week and loved it. The whining goes on. You tell him to eat up, mentioning casually that there's lovely pudding. He doesn't eat up, and you get that sinking feeling that confrontation is imminent. It looks like deadlock, and it is.

At this point mothers plumb the depths of cunning. Our honour, pride, self-respect are all at stake. *But so are the child's.* So instead of getting cross and telling him he can sit there until he eats every bite (he'll sit till Doomsday if he's the confident, intelligent child you hope he is), you tell him sweetly that of course he doesn't have to eat it *if he's not hungry*. Note: you are not admitting for an instant that he doesn't like it – he's just not hungry for it. His reaction to this unexpected, apparent capitulation on your part will usually give you the clue you're looking for. If he looks baffled and rather annoyed, the odds are that he has merely been trying you on. So call his bluff by withholding pudding, *or anything else*, until he eats at least enough of the meat to satisfy your honour. (Not necessarily the whole plateful.) Obviously no one must be allowed to gloat over him or tease him – half the battle with a food fad is saving his face along with your own.

On the other hand, if he looks relieved, or registers no further interest, then he's probably genuinely not hungry. But the same formula applies: no pudding. And if uproar breaks out *don't give an inch.* Children have a refined sense of justice from an early age. Even a toddler can grasp the logic of the argument. If he can't, or won't, that's his problem. Ours is to sidestep trouble at meals, and faddiness spreads like an epidemic through a family if the kids don't get preventive treatment. Anyway, kids *want* to respect their mothers. They find out if we are worthy of it by testing our nerve at meals.

It is the consensus of opinion among mothers we consulted that another rule worth establishing is that everyone must have a bit of everything going – and that includes mum, even if she is known far and wide as a cabbage-hater. A teaspoonful is enough to make the point. If the children grumble and groan, remember you're a mother, not a mouse. There'll be plenty of time for spoiling when you're a grandmother.

For those who think this is a policy of perfection unsuitable for the progressive age we live in, it's fair to say that judicious compromise comes into it. Allowing each child in a family to have one, and only one pet hate that he is never made to eat, nor even offered, can give a lot of leverage in persuading him to eat everything else.

But food fads are made as well as born; here we come up against one of the thorniest problems of motherhood. Nothing makes a child fussier, faddier or more difficult over food than the mother who is constantly prodding him to eat. We all do it; and learn the hard way that it is counter-productive. Every mother has an inner compulsion to stuff her child with healthy food, and some of us have an added compulsion: a social conscience born of war and postwar rationing in days when wasting food was a crime against life itself. Watching a child eat half a banana and abandon the rest is an outrage to a mum who never clapped eyes upon, let alone ate a banana in early childhood because there *were* no bananas. We're all uncomfortably aware that a majority of children in the world don't get enough to eat – throwing away a meal half-eaten makes us feel guilty and bad-tempered: eating it ourselves makes us bad-tempered and fat.

But pressure, in whatever circumstances, is a recipe for recurrent trouble at meals. Mild encouragement is all a child will take. We must encourage, for many kids are actually very lazy about eating and would rather not make the effort to chew, even if they like what they have on their plates. But look at it from the child's point of view. A four-year-old couldn't care less about food values and vitamins: all he knows is that Big Mother is standing over him pestering him to eat his food. He's not crazy about this particular meal, and it has to be chewed, too. But his own metabolism might persuade him to eat if Big Mother would only shut up and let him get on with it. He'll be slow, and that's irritating, but with the minimum encouragement he'll get there by himself.

It takes willpower and patience to avoid bringing pressure, but there's more to it than that. Estimating how much a child will eat, or ought to eat, is always tricky, but we won't go far wrong if we cook a little less than we reckon is enough. If it's too little, we'll hear all about it soon enough and know for next time. And mild encouragement takes a variety of forms. A reluctant eater can be helped along with a timely suggestion that he might like some ketchup with his meat, or butter on his sprouts – or mayonnaise, or *anything*, no matter how eccentric, that his mother knows he likes. One mum sprinkles coloured sugar strands on cauliflower; another gets through a bottle of ketchup in four days; another has become such an expert in disguising food that half the time she forgets, herself, just what it is she cooked. It doesn't matter which ruse we employ: the only thing that matters is that our children enjoy meals and mealtimes and stay friends with us.

But there is a hard core of children who persist with faddiness for years, apparently impervious to guile. The older the child, the harder it is to outwit him, anyway. It becomes more difficult to disguise the food, to hide our motives, to call his bluff – if it *is* bluff, and the older the child the harder it is to tell. Assuming that no medical problem is involved, you still have a couple of tricks up your sleeve. No child, at any age, is going to die or incur any damage whatever if he skips a meal. Or even two meals. Any child over two can do without food for a day, or longer. If your child is being so impossible about food that you despair of your ability to get him through the next meal without murdering him, just don't give him the next meal. Don't give him *anything*, except drinks, and see what happens. However proud or stubborn, he will be more flabbergasted than he lets on; the ritual of meals is as sacred to him as it is to his mother. He might hold out for one meal, seldom more. When he hangs round the door looking sulky, suggest easily that he might like a bite or two. If he stamps off in a huff, leave it till he comes round. *No* snacks, *no* little extras, *no* running next door for a handout. Sometimes the fastest way to find out whether a child from three years old onwards is bluffing you with food fads is to ring his best friend's mum and enlist her support. Maybe he's eating food in her house that he won't touch at home. How you handle the evidence is up to you, but the casual approach is more effective than a whip over the head in front of the whole family.

As a postscript on faddiness we must spotlight a specific fad which, along with green vegetables, is commonest and most infuriating of all. Eggs mean a lot to mothers. Beautifully packaged, the symbol of all things good, the egg can be the cause of more friction between mothers and children than anything except sweets. A very few children can't eat eggs. Most can and will, but a high proportion get faddy about them in some form at some time. Overnight a child used to eggs from babyhood may declare that soft-boiled eggs make him feel sick; and he may well be telling the truth. We can hard-boil, we can scramble, we can bake – sometimes nothing works. He's just gone off eggs for the time being. If you feel strongly about them you are in for a lot of effort disguising them. Or you could just write it off to experience, and remember that an egg deficiency never lost anyone votes.

**Fat**

Ask anyone just home from a church or village fête who won the Bonny Baby contest – you can bet it was the fattest baby. Now ask the doctor at the baby clinic what, in his view, is his greatest single headache in dealing with mothers – we'll bet that it's mothers who overfeed their children. The medical profession is trying hard to get across to the public that overeating and overweight can start in babyhood and childhood, but most of us still think it's an adult problem. It is, but it's a child's problem too.

It's one thing to be a bonny baby, but since the days of Billy Bunter the fat child has been a target for laughs. The fat child doesn't think it's funny. It's no fun to be slow at games, to be called Fatty or Podge, to be left out of things. Children under the age of perhaps seven may not notice that one of their friends is a heavyweight, but after that age they may start to giggle and jeer. A child may feel too miserable about it even to tell his mother. He is quite likely to eat more, to comfort himself. And so it goes on.

It's not fair; and it may be our fault. Every mother is proud when her baby gains weight; she worries when he doesn't. Most of us give our babies all they will take, and haven't the heart to reduce the intake of the baby who loves his food, grabs all he can, and gets too fat accordingly. Some babies slim down when they start to move around and burn up their calories; some don't. A baby who goes through his first years at an average weight, or even a skinny baby who ran his mother ragged over feeding problems during babyhood, may turn into the fatty of Primary Three. Very common is the child who is a carbon copy of fat mum or fat dad – or both. Even more obvious and most common of all is the child who is overweight simply because he has a huge appetite and loves rich, fattening foods.

In other words, some kids have a tendency to plumpness anyway, and some don't – but have mothers who allow or encourage them to eat far more than they need. If you think your child is overweight, the first step is to find out why. If you can get rid of the reason for it, the weight problem may gradually sort itself out without further action on your part. Children are overweight for most of the same reasons that make adults overweight: stress, boredom, an overlarge appetite, hereditary tendencies they are stuck with from birth. Many children stay solid and sturdy right through childhood but could not be described as overweight. An easygoing, unenergetic child uses up fewer calories than a reckless tree-climber who eats as much or more. A seven or eight-year-old, tense and scared of school, may overeat for comfort. A bored, or lonely, or privately unhappy child may do the same. *Whatever reason you think it may be, check with your doctor.*

Glandular problems are rare, but it might be glands. Or there might be a psychological problem that may require treatment not even a mother can give. In any case, if a mother plans to reduce her child's weight by dieting, the doctor should know all about it and be asked for advice.

It goes without saying that the mother's attitude, in helping the overweight child, is almost more important than anything else. The child must on no account become anxious about his size – and if he's anxious already it is up to his mum to reassure him and keep his confidence boosted. A private talk with the doctor might usefully be followed by the doctor seeing the child on his own. Or you might invent some reason other than the child's overweight to take him to see the doctor, to keep the child's cool intact. Medical reasons for overweight are not part of our brief here, so we'll stick to the assumption that the diagnosis is simple overeating, or overfeeding by a persuasive or thoughtless mum. It can be quite a surprise. But better a blow to our ego than the discovery that the child's overweight is a symptom of something far more worrying than over-indulgence.

A doctor may recommend a specific diet, or he may merely tell us to give the child less to eat. Either way it's a problem in itself. Dieting is hard for anybody, most of all for a child. If he doesn't mind that he's fat – and on the whole you hope he *is* relaxed about it – he can't see why he should go without favourite foods like sweets, puddings, biscuits and bread and jam. If he does mind he is more likely to co-operate, but you may have added problems of self-consciousness and shyness. The older the child the higher the hopes for co-operation. Younger children can't be expected to see the point meal in meal out. It's a struggle for mum as well as the dieter.

Cutting down on carbohydrates is the obvious and most effective way to diet, but it is both unhealthy and unreasonable to cut out all fattening foods. The trick is to ease them off gradually until the child is getting only a spoonful of potato, an apple instead of pudding, one square of chocolate instead of four. (Half the battle of dieting is training the system both to eat less and to do without overdoses of carbohydrate.) A growing child should eat perfectly normally in every other way: milk, green vegetables, fruit, all the protein foods like meat, chicken, and fish, if possible served in the same way as the rest of the family gets them. Special diet menus call attention to the child and his problem and can embarrass him, let alone make the other kids feel resentful at the special attention Harry is getting. It's hard on everybody, because it's almost impossible to keep one child off the richer foods if other kids are having them. Dieting a child means keeping temptation out of his way, which inevitably means keeping it out of everybody's way. Otherwise it's not fair –

and the fat child who feels hard done by is quite likely to crave cake and sweets all the more and cheat when he can. Adults, it should be said, do just the same – and we're supposed to have willpower.

Apart from careful feeding, what else can a mother do to help? Encouragement and praise may not be enough. A little girl who has been invited to be a bridesmaid in a couple of months may be motivated to slim for the wedding. A little boy might be lured along by the promise of new football boots for the coming season. But extra concentration on keeping the child happy at home and at school is more important than promises of treats or rewards. If the child's teachers can be asked to co-operate, and school meals quietly adjusted for him, so much the better, provided it can be done without any kind of fuss.

A child who is prone to fat may have the problem all his life, so even when he reaches a normal weight his mother should not let the diet regime lapse entirely. Retraining eating habits takes a long time and requires constant watching. But equally the child should not be allowed to get fanatical about his figure to the point where he can't, or won't, eat as much as he needs to keep well. (Teenage girls can be very silly about dieting, for example, and just occasionally a case of silliness can become a medical case and be very alarming.) Whatever the diet programme, and for whatever reason, no child should lose weight too fast. A pound a week is plenty. And any child on a diet should be supervised by a doctor as well as by his mother.

And when all is said and done, nearly every word can be applied to overweight adults as much as to overweight children. It helps to remember that the family who stuffs together may have to slim together.

### Frail

One mother we know, asked to tell us what she meant by a 'frail' child, produced a collection of photographs of herself as a child and passed them around. There she was, pale and peaky of face, thread-like of limb, up to the age of ten. The later pictures showed an astonishing transformation. Over the next couple of years she turned into quite a plump, rosy little girl whom nobody could possibly describe as frail or even on the skinny side. It wasn't a matter of delicate health that suddenly improved, she said; she was healthy all the way. She just *looked* terrible.

Skinny kids are skinny for a lot of the same reasons, in reverse, why fat kids are fat. They can be born that way; it can run in the family; a child can be tense, nervous, unhappy, or depressed and lose his appetite instead of eating for comfort. A lot of frail-looking children have normal, even large appetites but burn up their calories in energetic or restless behaviour. Some children stay thin or get thin because they actively dislike rich foods, preferring to live on what most of us would call a slimming diet. And of course, too much pressure to eat is the classic reason for a child, whether thin or not, losing his appetite and going off his food. If you're baffled, or worried, or both – see your doctor.

But the child who is ill or convalescing is the commonest example of frailty and the one which concerns us most often. Wooing back a lost appetite can be extremely difficult, even nerve-racking, for a mother already nervous over a child's health. This is the problem we'll concentrate on here.

Sick children don't and won't eat, nor are they expected to. We should mentally subtract years from a child's actual age when he is ill; his natural reaction to feeling rotten is to revert to babyhood, where nothing is expected of him and he receives maximum coddling. (Many an adult does the same in similar circumstances, and many a mother would love to.) The more severe the illness, the greater the loss of appetite is likely to be: lack of interest in food can persist well beyond the convalescent stage and even when a child is pronounced fit he may still look thin and spindly. It's worrying, but there's a lot we can do early on to save us more worry later.

Since the convalescent child still feels like a baby, he might be started on the road back to normal eating with baby foods. All those little tins of bone-and-vegetable broth, chicken-

and-rice dinner and the array of puddings and strained fruits come back into their own. Sloppy cereals and custards in tiny amounts might get him going; after that the tins are invaluable. There is absolutely no point in cooking little attractions for him yourself – in the first place you run the risk of being doubly disappointed if he won't eat them and in the second place you need all your strength to get up the stairs, let alone look after the rest of the family. Looking after *you* is just as important as looking after an ailing child. He's going to be whiny, he's going to be bored and cross, especially when he starts getting better. Breaking your heart and your back over food he may or may not touch is an added burden at a time when you may be tired and anxious and ready to snap at somebody, maybe even him. It's not worth it. Apart from pre-cooked baby foods, there's a lot to be said for one mother's suggestion for sustaining a sick child successfully: glucose for him; gin for mum.

When a convalescent makes progress in eating to the point where you dare to think in terms of ordinary food again, the gentle, casual approach is just as important. If you're lucky, the child might ask for something himself. If he doesn't, you might tell him what the rest of the family are having and suggest that he might like a little. Or offer him a few options, to get him interested. Sometimes a child recovering at home, up and around at last, will revive enthusiasm for food if his mother asks him to help in the cooking. Any kind of gimmick may help, provided it's simple and doesn't involve a lot of effort on your part. Falling over backwards to make fancy rabbit moulds can alert a child to the fact that mum is worried sick that he's off his food; he is quite likely to cultivate the worry to stay in the spotlight of attention.

Serving food to a child with little appetite is as important as the food itself. A dab or two on a small plate can develop into larger dabs on a big plate – both *look* the same to a small child. An older child might be inspired to eat if you serve a meal to him in a baking tin – the kind with individual compartments for baking buns. A little meat in one, a little vegetable in another, some potato, some pudding, a piece of apple, a few small sweets and before he stops to think about it he has eaten the lot. Maybe he's still not very interested in the food, but he's entertained by the idea. Even milk tastes better out of a straw, and a box of coloured straws bought specially for him can distract a child's attention. Maybe he won't notice the egg beaten into the milk.

Usual rules about eating between meals should obviously be suspended for the duration – within reason. It's only fair that a child being coaxed back to good health and normal eating deserves special privileges over food, and if there are rumbles of discontent among the other children that's only fair, too. We've found that sympathizing and agreeing with our children about life's little injustices can go a long way. Some things *aren't* fair. Being sick isn't fair, and sometimes being the mother of a frail child can seem unfairest of all.

**Sweets**

Sweets – and we don't mean puddings, but chocolate, candies, acid drops, and mints without or with holes – are bad for teeth, appetite, and budget. There isn't a self-respecting dentist, doctor, or household economist who would not agree. The problem for mothers is that kids love them. More than that: kids will get them and eat them no matter how hard we try to prevent it.

This is not to say that mothers should throw in the towel, abandon the unequal struggle and let cavities take their course. It merely means that, though sweets are always with us like Rising Prices and Race Relations, rules about them can't succeed if restrictions are too rigid. It is entirely possible, if we try hard enough, to keep a child off sweets altogether up to the age of five or six by never having sweets in the house, telling all friends and relations never to produce them nor even mention them, and rigorously confiscating any that appear with visiting children. But a total ban inevitably breaks down as the child gains independence and pocket money – and you can bet that the child denied sweets from birth will be first in the queue at the candy counter. We think that prohibition leads to more trouble in the end.

But rules can be made and kept if they are reasonable. The only worthwhile test of a family rule about sweets is – does it work? Here are some policies pursued by mothers who feel as strongly about sweets as any dentist. Each has been in operation for several years and each mother claims at least partial success.

Family A has sweets only at weekends. Family B is allowed sweets (not more than two) after meals, followed by a general exodus to brush teeth. Family C can eat as many sweets as they want after supper and *at no other time* – they then brush their teeth before bed. Family D have been trained to like apple and pieces of carrot after meals and their mother says they sneer at any sweet offered to them. (We are bound to say that we have not actually seen this happen, but it's a beautiful thought.) Family E have no hard and fast rules, but their mother has dental problems herself, keeps a tight eye on her children's teeth and dishes out sweets sparingly at odd intervals. Family F have had fluoride tablets every day from birth, still have them in adolescence, and have been taught to think of sweets as pure poison – they ate them as young children but tailed off as they grew older and wiser.

If you feel you need a policy, or if the policy you have isn't working, try one of these and see how it goes. If it works, it's good. But along with a reasonable attitude towards sweet-eating it is important to get across some propaganda about the damage that can be done to both first and second teeth (to say nothing of face and figure) by too many sweets too casually absorbed. If the kids go regularly to the dentist, and especially if they get along well with him, they are likely to swallow this sort of propaganda more readily from him than from mum. When children are encouraged from early childhood to regard sweets as dangerous as well as delicious, they are brought at least part of the way towards consciousness and care of their own teeth – instead of mum doing all the thinking for them.

It is probably too much to suggest that sweet advertising might be restricted, as cigarette advertising has been, but resistance to this area of temptation can be built up at home.

It takes effort. New confections accompanied by catchy jingles are the nightmare of a mother trying to establish sensible rules about sweets – particularly when the housekeeping is fully stretched anyway. It's hard to keep saying no, no to the child who skids into the kitchen, punch-drunk from the blandishments of television advertisements, to beg for the newest chew. It takes a lot of willpower and resistance at the supermarket check-out point, where sweets are temptingly displayed to attract the child fed up and bored with shopping. One way and another we find that outside influences are almost invariably bad – even teachers have been known to end a week at school with sweeties all round before the kids go home, and some indulgent grannies seem to regard sweets as the only legal currency.

We can't win all the time, and it's probably better that we shouldn't. In any case it's fair to say that some sweets are worse than others. Lollipops and boiled sweets lovingly sucked over long periods are especially bad for the teeth. So are gluey, chewy toffees and candy bars. Chocolate, on the other hand, contains iron and isn't quite so potentially damaging.

But perhaps the worst thing of all about sweets is not that children eat too many and stand to wreck their teeth and/or appetites. It is rather that we ourselves – hard-pressed mothers – can very easily fall into the habit of using sweets to smooth things over. Promising a sweet to the first child who eats up his vegetables is using sweets as reward. Running to the candy jar when a child comes roaring in with a grazed knee is using sweets as compensation. Either of these can only be called a Bad Thing. Whatever reasonable and flexible rules about sweets we adopt, they should not include the ruse of giving a child some chocolate drops to keep him quiet while we read the paper – this is peace bought at too high a price. The pernicious part is that such ruses work – for a short time. After that, like bribery, they backfire.

# 8 Dads only

The fact that mum is going to be away from home for a time doesn't mean that dad is going to be left high and dry, on the rocks, unable to cope – not a bit of it. Of course you can cope. Remember all the times you've said: 'There's nothing to this housekeeping nonsense, it's just that women make such a fuss about it', and (much louder) 'What this house needs is a little systematic thinking'. Of course you remember.

And you should go on saying it, out loud, several times a day while mum isn't there. You may find it useful to read some of the suggestions offered here, too. Then when your wife returns with the new baby, or having got granny over her fractured hip, or with that evanescent health farm bloom, the kitchen may not be a chaos of carbonized egg and decaying fragments of fish fingers.

Nervous mothers should note here that our suggestions, though a far cry from the way orthodox mums run homes and children, are designed especially for fathers left in charge on their own. The first objective is to keep mum assured at long distance that all is well. There can be few things more worrying than having to leave the family, for whatever reason, in a fret that dad will find it hard to manage or – worse – manage but be miserable. New babies come; emergencies arise; mum can even come down with a bad case of measles. There are times when dad *has* to cope.

It's fair to assume that dad is left in charge of school-age children – four or five-plus. (Toddlers and babies require full-time attention from a full-time emergency source.) This chapter is a checklist for dads coping alone on that basis. It starts with the last glimpse of your wife's face as she is whirled away on the train/taxi/hospital trolley, and ends at the moment when, having kissed and counted noses all round, she turns to you and says 'You never told me Janie had a cold'.

Whether her absence is for three days or three weeks, it will probably feel like thirty years. The notions here may make the sentence pass, if not more quickly, at least more smoothly. We can only add that we've never lost a father yet.

**'I did it my way . . .'**

Set up your own routine. You're in charge now, so act that way. If you try to follow mum's routine, or what you think was her routine, there'll be trouble at once.

In the first place you'll find out the hard way that what took her twenty minutes will take you an hour and make twice the mess. In the second place the children will notice immediately that dad trying to be mum is different from mum being mum, and they won't like it. They like dad to be dad, warts and all. So gather up into a tidy pile the pages and pages of detailed instructions mum left on the kitchen table, and put them away in a drawer. You might glance at them once in a while, in case they say 'Don't let David put on his eczema ointment by himself – he likes the taste', but by and large you can feel free to play things your way.

It is both wiser and easier to recognize that, from the moment mum leaves, home life will be different from the norm. There will be a general air of change, so *use* it. A change can be as good as a holiday, and the children may be so intrigued by it that you can engage and keep their co-operation. The only thing that shouldn't change is bedtime – bedtimes should stay the same or even earlier. Don't put up with any whining or monkey business over this one. You need time on your own in the evening, heaven knows.

### 'Jobs for the boys . . .'

Give a child a task and you give him a sense of importance. Anybody *over five* can make a bed (more or less); set a table (with the forks on the wrong side, but so what); hang up coats and pyjamas and bring in scattered toys and bikes from the garden. Anybody *over eight* can dress anybody under five (provided the under-five has been consulted on the matter and sees that it is in the public interest); clear and stack plates and empty kitchen rubbish into the dustbin. If everyone in the family has his own job to do for the duration, and knows it, there's a good chance that he will stick to it and not forget more than once or twice.

A vital point is that all the kids should get everything ready for school *the night before*. It saves a lot of panic in the morning if satchels, gym shoes, homework books, everything they're going to need for school is laid out ready for the 'off'.

But dad's main problem may well be one of channelling the energies of over-enthusiastic helpers into safe, yet satisfying jobs. It's a good idea to keep a mental list of alternatives ready, so that when a ten-year-old offers to saw the legs off the kitchen stool to stop it wobbling, you can side-track him into sweeping out the garage instead.

No child under eight should be expected or allowed to do more than the simplest shopping – two or three items only, and then *only if there are no roads to cross*. Better go without than risk an accident. Children over ten or eleven may do some unsupervised cooking, but *only* an older child famed far and wide for reliability and caution. On the other hand the most slap-happy seven-year-old can wash a lettuce, especially if you tell him he might disturb a slug or two. Dads in charge would be well advised to ban all access to the stove for the duration. You'll do better getting to grips with that capricious beast on your own.

**'The daily round, the common task . . .'**

Tidiness is better than cleanliness, and godliness is nowhere. Tidy once and furiously each day and make the children help *before* television, or any other attraction. (Food is not an attraction.) A tidy house steadies a tired dad's nerves more effectively than a clean one; but if you have to clean, then choose a Saturday morning when everyone is at home to help. Give each child a duster or a damp cloth and a fixed number of items each to clean; then somebody over eight can get out a carpet sweeper or vacuum cleaner to do the floors. Bedrooms matter less than living rooms. Bathroom floors should be dried, and the towels hung up. The kitchen floor has priority, because if that gets ignored for longer than a couple of days it will get both messy and slippery and the kids will tread the gunk from the kitchen floor on to the living room floor. That is if they don't slip and fall first – and there are a lot of sharp edges to fall against in a kitchen.

Note and remember the locations of clean drying-up cloths, clean towels, spare soap, toothpaste, and lavatory paper – it can be a real disaster to run out. Since there is usually one child in a family who has a particularly beady eye and knows where things are, make that child responsible for alerting you to potential shortages. Be sure you know where the nail scissors are, where the shampoo, sticking plaster, and disinfectant are kept, where the shoe-cleaning equipment lives. Don't, whatever you do, accept any offers from young children (that is, kids under about nine or ten) to clean their own shoes. The resulting shoe polish stains on skin and clothes will be a nightmare – not even acres of newspaper and enveloping aprons will prevent the stuff smearing from here to eternity. Save shoe-cleaning as a private job for dad during the 9 o'clock news – once, if possible, before mum returns.

### 'Bubble, bubble, toil and trouble . . .'

Children get through clean clothes at frightful speed and so do dads. In our view it is a waste of time and breath to pester kids to keep their clothes clean. Many a mum does it, but while mum is away this particular nag is bad for the kids' morale, and yours. (Save your nags for when you really need them.) The fact remains that it takes a daunting amount of time and labour to keep a family in clean clothes, and dads coping alone are more than justified in using every available short cut. You can maintain a steady supply of clean socks and smalls, for example, by letting the children wash these themselves in the bath. Bubble bath liquid washes everything and everybody and you get a ringless bath as a bonus. (Detergent liquid does the same, rather cheaper, but watch carefully for skin reaction and stop instantly if you notice a rash.)

Establish a basket or box at a focal point into which all large-scale dirty clothes can be dumped, and don't let the pile get too high before taking them to the launderette. Washing clothes at home is fine if ideal conditions prevail – ideal means a foolproof washing machine and a guaranteed way of getting wet clothes dry. Commercial dryers are large, powerful, and good for everything except nylon, but ask advice from the supervisor at the launderette to be sure. She may take pity on you and take charge of the whole boring business.

Ironing can go by the board, but you may get stuck with having to press blouses, shirt fronts and cuffs, the skirts of dresses; the bits that *show*. Never underwear, never nightwear, and never let anybody under twelve go near the iron. Many a dad doesn't know that it takes a long time to *cool down*, besides being a dangerous object in use. Store it upright on a heatproof surface, well out of reach.

As for your own shirts, either have them professionally

laundered (expensive); wash them yourself and iron only the necessary bits (tiresome); or buy two nylon ones and drip-dry them over the bath on alternate nights (satisfactory). Abandon all handkerchiefs in favour of paper tissues all round. Likewise make sure you have a good supply of kitchen paper rolls for use as table napkins and for wiping up spills anywhere, any time.

Rather than changing and washing sheets every week, turn them over to the reverse side and swing them top to bottom as well, so that this week's toes end becomes next week's pillow end. (The theory behind this is that children aren't tall enough to grubby up the bottom of a full-size bed.) Pillow cases can be turned inside out. If the beds in your house have continental quilts (with which you only need bottom sheets), now is the time to appreciate them as never before – they take all the work out of bed-making.

**'Make me an offer I can't refuse . . .'**

It nearly – not quite – goes without saying that dad coping on his own should accept, if not jump at, all offers of help from friendly neighbours. We have one or two reservations about the general beauty of the idea. The neighbour who will child-mind can be a godsend, certainly, but it doesn't do to stretch goodwill too far. Besides the possibility that she may get fed up with the arrangement before dad does, there is a more critical consideration.

Most kids, especially small ones, prefer to be home with dad while mum is away, even if dad *is* rushed off his feet and home is on the topsy-turvy side. A child parked for longish periods in different households during his mother's absence can easily feel pushed out of the way or even – at worst – actually abandoned. The more a child is involved in activities at home, and the closer he feels to his family at this time, the more cheerful and co-operative he is likely to be and *the less likely he is to play up when mum gets back*. The real test of how well dad has coped on his own – we think it's the only test – is whether or not the kids take it out on mum afterwards. She feels bad at having to leave them at all, and she'll expect them to blame her in one way or another. If they play her up only a little, and it passes quickly, then dad deserves all praise and honour. It's the hallmark of success.

If offers of help are thick on the ground it's useful to ask a neighbour to pay the milkman weekly, or whenever he comes for the money – it's the kind of thing you forget until he materializes on the doorstep just after you have run out of cash. Don't, please, forget to ask the nice neighbour what you owe *her*. A friendly soul who offers to do some shopping can be a great help too, provided you don't give her *carte blanche* along with the money and leave the shopping to her imagination. Give her a list of what *you* want, or she will bring you what *she* thinks you'll want. (It's no use being confronted with, say, knuckle-of-veal if you don't know how to cook it and haven't time to find out.) When you buy fresh meat, make it mince: 100 g (¼ lb) per head is a fair guide to quantity.

### 'Which brings us to food . . .'

Your basic shopping list includes bread, eggs, bacon, sausages, breakfast cereal, potatoes, butter, marge, and fruit, especially apples and bananas. If your fridge has a compartment to keep frozen stuff frozen, then get a lot of ice-cream – vanilla is a safe bet. A box of ice-cream cones never comes amiss; and neither does a can or two of beer for you. Thus fortified, here follows a golden maxim which every dad-in-charge can cling to when it comes to food for the family.

### Never be afraid of unorthodox meals

You're the boss. Now's your chance – and the children's – to have fried bread with marmalade if you want it; crisps for breakfast; no green veg. Outraged mothers who may have strayed into this chapter will know that it is well-nigh impossible to ruin, especially during a short period of time, the well-balanced eating habits of children who have been on a sensible diet all their short lives. It won't happen. The kids won't *let* it happen. To the mum who objects on the grounds that *her* child will eat sweets, cake, and biscuits ad infinitum, let it be said that a child will only do this if there is *literally nothing else* between him and starvation. No child will eat sweet things exclusively for longer than a day or two if there's so much as a sniff of another option, such as a cheese sandwich.

Variety, as eccentric as you care to make it, is the important ingredient. So let's take meals through breakfast and high tea and see what they look like with short cuts and practical advice mixed into them. Meals for weekends come along in a minute and include a midday meal, which sounds alarming but is actually less so because you've got more time. During the week dad's worst headache is not inexperience but the inexorable pressure of the school timetable on the household – everything is a race against the clock. We'll assume that the kids have a meal at school on weekdays; we hope that you have a good working can opener; and we beg you to make up your mind here and now that you're never going to use more than three pans per meal *and wash them up as you go along*.

**Breakfast**

Breakfast starts the night before, after the children have gone to bed. Set the table and pour breakfast cereal into each bowl at night, short-circuiting any dawn arguments about what kind the kids fancy. Decide what, if anything, you're going to cook, bearing in mind another golden rule for dads, *never fry*. Frying is messy and spitty and you have to stand over it during the cooking: grill or bake instead, and put away the frying pan until mum comes home.

Boiled eggs are the easiest cooked breakfast (remember to take them out of the fridge the night before); and so are bacon or sausages baked with tomatoes:

1 or 2 sausages or bacon rashers per person
½ a tomato per person
a few small knobs of butter

Cut the sausages in half, or the rashers into bite-sized bits, with kitchen scissors. Lay these in a shallow ovenproof dish or baking tin and put in the tomatoes with the cut side up and knobs of butter on top.

Get it ready the night before. In the morning turn on the oven first thing, and heat it to 350°F (180°C or gas 4). Bake the bacon and tomatoes for 15-20 minutes.

So a morning routine for dads might look something like this. Get up a little earlier than usual and briefly practise a confident smile in front of the mirror while you shave. Now turn on the oven (if you're doing the bake) or put on a pan of water to boil (if you're doing boiled eggs). Bound upstairs to wake the children and start them getting dressed, then downstairs again to boil or bake. With a little luck breakfast should bowl along fairly smoothly, but you will be amazed at the amount of washing-up it generates. Stack the dishes in soapy water if you haven't time to do them until later, and don't forget to turn off the oven.

After breakfast politely ask the kids to go back upstairs to wash their faces and brush their teeth and hair. Anybody who can make his bed should do it now, and everybody picks up their pyjamas. Inspect them and send one child back upstairs to brush again, just to show them that you mean business. (Don't feel you have to do this every morning – it's just that spot checks keep the kids up to scratch and show them that dad is in control.) Get them into their coats for school and tell each one how good and helpful he has been. They probably have been, especially if dad has stayed calm and cheerful and remembered to bracket his instructions with please and thank you. It may sound like a lot of nonsense to remind busy dads about good manners, but they act as a magic oil to lubricate the jerky progress of domestic wheels, let alone pour on troubled waters.

It's not likely that you'll have either time or inclination to plan food for later in the day, but if a kind neighbour is doing some shopping for you she will need a list. Post it through her letterbox as you leave in the morning. Otherwise think about food in your lunch hour and shop on the way home. If the idea of preparing a meal in the evening turns your thought processes to stone, remember that you can always produce breakfast in reverse order – savoury first and cereal last – and call it supper. But a judicious balance of tinned and fresh foods can add up to very simple, very satisfactory evening meals with no echo of the orphanage about them and very little effort on dad's part. Here are five to carry you through the school and working week.

### Monday

½ a large tin (411 g or 14½ oz) of spaghetti-in-tomato-sauce per person
250 g (8 oz) grated Cheddar cheese
1 banana and 1 apple per person, for pudding

Make the pudding first, peeling and chopping the fruit and mixing it all together. A squeeze of lemon juice from a plastic lemon will stop the fruit going brown. Now heat the spaghetti and mix the cheese into it, stirring with a wooden spoon to prevent sticking. Meanwhile the children can lay the table, wash their hands, and *sit down.*

### Tuesday

½ a large tin (411 g or 14½ oz) mince per person
a packet or two of instant potato mix
oranges for pudding

Heat the oven to 350°F (180°C or gas 4). Pour the mince into a heatproof casserole or oven dish. Make up the potato according to the instructions on the packet and spread this over the top of the meat. Bake for 20-25 minutes while you peel the oranges and break them into segments. Put these in a bowl and give each child a plate with a little mound of sugar on it to dip the segments into at pudding time.

### Wednesday

tinned vegetable soup
tinned or ready-cooked cold meats (corned beef, ham, meat loaf, salami)
sliced hard-boiled eggs
sliced tomatoes
yoghurt for pudding

Slice the meats and arrange them with the egg and tomato on a large flat dish to serve with ketchup or bottled mayonnaise. Heat up the soup slowly over low heat and serve it first with buttered toast – not too much, or the kids won't eat the main course. Finish up with yoghurt all round.

### Thursday

½ a large tin (411 g or 14½ oz) of meat balls per person
1 or 2 large packets of crisps
ice-cream and fresh green grapes for pudding

Heat the oven to 350°F (180°C or gas 4). Put the crisps in an ovenproof dish and heat them through for about 15 minutes. Wash the grapes and put these in a bowl (nobody gets any until supper is over). Pour the meat balls into a pan, heat them through slowly over low heat and serve them in bowls with the crisps scattered on top. Finally dish out the ice-cream and let the kids squabble over who grabbed the most grapes.

### Friday

fish and chips bought on the way home
tinned mandarin oranges for pudding

Wrap the fish in foil and keep hot in a low oven, 200°F (100°C or gas ¼). Spread the chips out in a large shallow baking tin and keep these hot too – they will get a little dry, but it doesn't matter.

Now none of these meals is going to get dad a Cordon Bleu certificate as a cook, but they're pretty impressive, besides being impressively simple. They are proper meals – not catch-as-catch-can affairs between homework and bedtime, and any dad can be proud of them. The key to success is timing. Aim at serving supper by 6 o'clock; earlier if possible. If smaller children can be got ready for bed before they eat, so much the better. And, just as it is reasonable to insist that homework and any chores must be done before television or games take over, so it is reasonable to insist that high tea or supper take place in a civilized manner. Clean hands. Brushed hair. Lots of pleases and thank yous. No jumping up and down from the table. This meal should be a high spot in the kids' day. There's a lot to talk about and they want to relax and enjoy it. So do you.

Weekends call for a midday meal two days running. We think this calls for the biggest chicken dad can lay his hands on – 2-2½ kg (4-5 lb) in weight, or 2 smaller ones if you're not sure. The trick is to cook seriously only *once*: hot chicken on Saturday and cold chicken on Sunday with hot baked potatoes to perk it up. When breakfast is over on Saturday morning and the kids are doing their household chores, dad should clear the decks in the kitchen and proceed as follows:

**Weekend wonder**

1 very large (or 2 smaller) chicken
1 (or 2) peeled onions
2 potatoes per person, peeled and quartered
a few sausages if you have them
3-4 (or 6-8) bacon rashers
a knob of marge or dripping
salt and pepper

Line a big roasting tin with a piece of foil large enough to fold over into a parcel. Place the chicken in the middle (if you're using two chickens make two separate parcels), making sure you have removed the gruesome assortment of giblets lurking in the breast cavity. Put a peeled onion in there instead. Lay the quartered potatoes around the chicken, and if you have some sausages you can cut these in half and put them around too. Drape bacon rashers over the breast of the bird and press the knob of marge or dripping onto the breastbone. Now fold the foil over and round the whole lot to form a fairly loose parcel. (The idea is to cook partly in juice, partly in steam.)

Meanwhile heat up the oven to 350°F (180°C or gas 4). At 10 a.m. put in the chicken parcel and leave it until 12.30 p.m. (If you're doing two smaller chicken parcels, put them in half an hour later.) At 12.30 p.m. turn the foil back and put the chicken with its trimmings back in the oven to brown until 1 o'clock. That leaves you half an hour to round up the children, lay the table, and heat up a can or two of carrots or peas. Carve the chicken in its foil straight on to plates, then fold over again and leave the remains parcelled up in the turned-off oven. If you have carved it cannily there may be enough for second helpings as well as for Sunday.

Baked potatoes (see page 44) and tinned sweetcorn go well with the cold chicken next day. Pudding can be ice-cream cones on Saturday and ice-cream in bowls, with chocolate sauce out of a tube, on Sunday. Or a tin of rice pudding hotted up while you eat the main course, served with a tin of apricots or cherries.

Weekend suppers can be sandwiches and soup; cheese and crackers with fruit; boiled eggs (if you didn't have them for breakfast that day) with mugs of hot cocoa. If, after a splendid midday meal, you take the kids out and get them exhausted with strenuous activity and jolly games, you should be able to count on an easy ride through to the early bedtime. It might even be the moment to tackle hair-washing, for which you'll need a stiff drink, a bottle of baby shampoo (which doesn't sting the eyes), and an absorbing movie on television. Dump the kids in the bath, one at a time, and when their hair is washed park them in front of the screen to dry off.

Finally a brief re-cap of essential straws to clutch at:

Do it your way, not mum's way
Give each child a job and you give him a sense of importance
Tidiness is better than cleanliness
Try not to run out of clean clothes
Accept most offers of help, but use your judgment
Don't be afraid of making unorthodox meals

Smile, praise; be proud of successes and laugh at mistakes. Mum will be home soon. Believe it or not, she probably can't wait to get back to it all.

Any dad left in charge soon realizes how exhausting and exasperating being a mum can be. But maybe he'll also notice how entertaining it is. And he might even begin to suspect that mum has the most rewarding job in the world. She probably has.

# Index